Putting Library Assessment Data to Work

Putting Library Assessment Data to Work

Selena Killick and Frankie Wilson

facet
publishing

Published by Facet Publishing,
7 Ridgmount Street, London WC1E 7AE
www.facetpublishing.co.uk

Facet Publishing is wholly owned by CILIP: the Library and Information Association.

British Library Cataloguing in Publication Data
A catalogue record for this book is available from the British Library.

ISBN 978-1-78330-220-8 (paperback)
ISBN 978-1-78330-221-5 (hardback)
ISBN 978-1-78330-222-2 (e-book)

First published 2019

Text printed on FSC accredited material.

Typeset from authors' files in 11/14 pt Elegant Garamond and Myriad Pro by Flagholme Publishing Services
Printed and made in Great Britain by CPI Group (UK) Ltd, Croydon, CR0 4YY

Dedication

To Paul, Mark and Benji
(the great men behind the great women)

Contents

List of figures and tables

Figures

Tables

List of case studies

Authors and contributors

Authors

Selena Killick is the Senior Library Manager responsible for Engagement and Insight at the Open University, UK. Her remit includes leading the insight strategy to understand customer needs, experiences, perceptions and expectations of the Library. Previous roles include the Research & Development Officer for Cranfield University Libraries with responsibility for quality, performance and benchmarking activities. In 2003 she was part of the team that introduced LibQUAL+ to the UK in partnership with the Association of Research Libraries. She is a member of the Board of the International Conference on Performance Measurement in Libraries and has previously supported the Library Assessment Conference. Selena regularly analyses, presents, publishes and advises libraries on an international basis on library assessment.

Dr Frankie Wilson is the Head of Assessment at the Bodleian Libraries, University of Oxford, UK. She provides strategic leadership for assessment throughout the Libraries, including training staff in assessment techniques, and designing and running assessment activities to prompt change. Her dual focus is using the most appropriate methods – quantitative, qualitative, UX – to bring the voice of users into the Libraries' decision-making process, and using insights gained from a decade as a liaison librarian to effectively present the Libraries' case to funders.

Frankie holds a Doctorate in the field of assessment, quality and culture change in academic libraries and continues to be an active researcher as well as a practitioner. She is a Chair of the Board of the International Conference on Performance Measurement in Libraries and a member of the Board of the Library Assessment Conference. She previously served on the International Federation of Library Associations Standing Committee on Statistics and Evaluation.

Contributors

Jackie Belanger is the Director of Assessment and Planning at the University of Washington Libraries in the USA. In this role, she leads the Libraries' assessment programme and develops assessments designed to improve the Libraries' services and resources and to communicate the value of the Libraries to stakeholders. Recent publications include work on critical assessment, assessing student learning outcomes and using assessment management systems.

Lauren Bjorn is currently the Strategy and Business Change Manager at the University of Nottingham Libraries, UK. Lauren's passion for data – both qualitative and quantitative – has driven the Libraries' smart, evidence-based decision making around service development and improvement since 2014. Her use of data visualisation has improved understanding of data across the department, opening peoples' minds to its impact and worth. In addition to her role as the department's data lead, Lauren manages the Libraries' strategic programme – co-ordinating, planning and overseeing the delivery of high stake, high impact projects.

Norman Boyd started late in libraries. After taking his first degree, he was Client Services manager in the London and South Eastern Library Region HQ, moving on to become Systems Librarian and Workshop Coordinator in Further Education and then onto Customer Service roles in Anglia Ruskin University Library, UK. His roles have all had interesting titles and remits, including the latest of User Experience and Quality Coordinator.

Michelle Breen is the Head of the Information Services Department in the Glucksman Library at the University of Limerick in Ireland (UL). As a member of the Library's management team, Michelle provides strategic input into the development and management of the Library and the creation of a culture of excellence in the provision of resources, facilities, expertise and services. Michelle worked as the Librarian, Administration at UL from 2011 to 2018 and in that role she conducted many assessment projects, working closely with the University's Deputy Librarian, Ciara McCaffrey. They have published work directly informed by assessment data in peer-reviewed journals, including *Portal, Libraries and the Academy* and the *New Review of Academic Librarianship*.

Simon Collins is the Information Specialist for the faculty of Science, Engineering and Computing within the Library and Learning Services directorate at Kingston University, UK. He has been managing the Library user survey for the last three years and also co-ordinates the Library and Learning Services Student Voice Action Plan populated from the Library user survey, National Student Survey and the University's level 5 survey. Along with colleagues, he spoke at the Higher Education Academy Surveys Conference 2017. He is also increasingly interested in user experience and ethnographic techniques to understand the students' needs and how the Library can be improved.

Emily Daly is Head of Assessment and User Experience at Duke University Libraries in Durham, NC, USA. She co-ordinates Duke Libraries' Assessment Team and plans and conducts user research related to the Libraries' website, as well as library services, collections and spaces. Emily also co-leads the Libraries' Digital Preservation and Publishing Program and helps co-ordinate the Libraries' web interfaces teams.

Sam Dick is currently an Internal Communications Manager at The Open University, UK, where she is passionately focused on employee voice and employee engagement. She is a strong advocate of reducing the assumptions we make and using data, evidence and insight to inform decision making, whilst working collaboratively with stakeholders to co-design better services. This ethos was essential in her previous role as a Senior Library Manager responsible for Quality and Insight at The Open University Library, where she was instrumental in establishing the Library Student Panel to work more collaboratively with students and to improve the impact of student voice.

Maggie Faber is the Assessment and Data Visualization Librarian at University of Washington Libraries in the USA. She helps analyse and communicate assessment results and library-related data with interactive dashboards and visualisations. She also collaborates with Libraries staff to design and implement a variety of assessment projects. Recent publications include 'Towards a Critical Assessment Practice' for *In the Library with the Lead Pipe* and presentations at the Library Assessment Conference.

Josie Field was the Graduate Trainee Library Assistant 2015–16 at the University of Bradford in the UK where she undertook a research project about use of a particular space in the library. She currently works as a software engineer for Sky and is still interested in research, particularly in the transformations of knowledge and learning in the digital era.

Hannah Fogg is currently Assistant Director in the University Library at Anglia Ruskin University, UK. She leads the teams delivering frontline services across campuses in Cambridge, Chelmsford and Peterborough, and is responsible for service areas including marketing and promotional activities, staff learning and development and the ongoing improvement of the user experience. Having started her career in law firm libraries, she worked in private higher education for a number of years, developing library and wider student support services in response to user need and using a range of survey tools and other methodologies to gain insights into individuals' experiences.

Vanya Gallimore is the Academic Liaison Team Manager at the University of York Library in the UK. Whilst at York, Vanya has taken a lead role in developing innovative solutions to effective engagement with academic departments. She carried out a large-scale UX project to understand the needs of academics and establishing annual action plans with academic departments. Prior to working at York, Vanya started her career in academic libraries at the University of Reading, before completing a Masters in Librarianship at the University of Sheffield and then working in a number of departmental libraries at the University of Oxford.

Sarah George has been a subject librarian at the University of Bradford in the UK for longer than she cares to remember. She currently supports Archaeology, Chemistry, Chemical Engineering, Forensics and Integrated Science. Previous to that she was a school librarian, special collections assistant, field archaeologist and the world's worst research assistant. She is a chartered librarian, senior fellow of the Higher Education Academy and national teaching fellow.

Kay Grieves is Engagement and Impact Manager at University Library Services, University of Sunderland, UK. Kay is particularly interested in strategic marketing principles, how they can support the nurturing of customer relationships and how through these relationships we can encourage engagement and generate valuable qualitative impact evidence. Kay and her team are also committed to developing new approaches to data visualisation. Kay is a member of the Relationship Management in Higher Education Libraries Steering Group, Chair of the Northern Collaboration Value and Impact Special Interest Group and a member of the SCONUL Communications Advisory Group.

Tamera Hanken has been at Xavier University of Louisiana, New Orleans, USA, since 2017. Previously, she was Head of Information Access and Resources at Singapore Management University; Director of Logistics and Resource Distribution at University of Nevada, Las Vegas, UNLV Libraries; and Manager of Library Operations and Technology at Tacoma Community College in Washington State. Current and former roles involve training and motivating staff to streamline processes, to undertake stakeholder analysis of their customer base and to engage their positions critically and creatively to effect innovative approaches to managing operations and services.

Emilie Hardman is Interim Head of the Institute Archives and Special Collections for the MIT Libraries at Massachusetts Institute of Technology in the USA. Previously, Emily served as Program Head for Special Collections at MIT, after eight years at Harvard University's Houghton Library where her last position was that of Head of Teaching, Learning and Digital Scholarship.

Steve Hiller has been a transformational and inclusive leader in the library assessment community for more than 25 years. He retired as director of assessment and planning at the University of Washington Libraries, USA in December 2017 and is now Strategic Analysis and Institutional Research Librarian (40% post-retirement). He developed and led a robust assessment programme that utilised a variety of quantitative and qualitative assessment methods, including the triennial survey for faculty and students, which has been running continuously since 1992. Steve has presented and published on a number of assessment-related topics including user needs assessment, survey design and analysis, library planning and performance metrics, articulating library value and developing organisational capacity for sustainable assessment.

Dr Starr Hoffman is the Director of Planning and Assessment at the University of Nevada, Las Vegas Libraries in the USA. In this role, Starr leads strategic planning and assessment across the Libraries to improve services and support decision making. Starr's scholarship on assessment planning and data inventories includes workshops at major national and international library conferences and her well-reviewed 2016 book, *Dynamic Research Support for Academic Libraries*. In her work, she draws on her expertise in data analysis, organisational development and higher education administration.

Helen Jamieson is currently Head of Student Engagement within Library and Learning Services at Edge Hill University, Lancashire, UK. Helen has worked in

Higher Education libraries for over 20 years with a keen interest in performance measurement and key performance indicators, user experience (UX) techniques and academic literacies. Her current role involves managing a centralised academic skills service supporting students to develop their academic writing and information literacy skills. Helen is currently completing a Post Graduate Certificate in Higher Education – her pedagogical research project is focusing on supporting first year students with their transition into Higher Education.

Reshma Khan formerly worked at the University of Bradford, UK, for 20 years. During her tenure, Reshma worked as Customer Services Manager within the library, leading a team of Library Assistants and managing the enquiry desk. Before this role, Reshma was Subject Librarian for the Faculty of Business and Law. Reshma holds a degree in Library and Information Studies from the Liverpool John Moores University and a PGC in Business Management from the University of Bradford.

Zsuzsa Koltay is Director of Communications at Cornell University Library, USA. She directed Cornell University Library's assessment unit and programme from 2008 to 2018. Her leadership experience spans a broad range of domains including strategic communication, assessment, electronic publishing, public services, system design, project and service development and space improvement. As an experienced speaker and author, she has contributed substantively to librarianship through original thinking, experimentation and partnerships. She holds a Masters in Library Science from Indiana University and a five-year university diploma and teaching certificate in English and Hungarian Studies from Debrecen University, Hungary.

Ciara McCaffrey (BA, MLIS) is the Deputy Librarian at the University of Limerick in Ireland. In this role she co-ordinates cross-library management processes, namely human resources, finance, quality, assessment, communications, legislative matters and library-wide projects. She leads the Library's performance assessment programme, is an advocate of evidence-based librarianship and has conducted practice-based research that is action-oriented, with the aim of improving library services and informing practice. She has held roles in a number of Irish university libraries in a career spanning 20 years.

Belinda Norman has worked in academic libraries and higher education for many years and is happiest working with collaborators on creative change. She has a passion for engaged and participatory approaches to connect people and make sure strategy and services are driven by the needs of client communities.

Davina Omar is Head of Academic Support at the University of West London (UWL), UK, and a member of the UWL Library Management team. She is the strategic lead for the Library's academic support to the University's Schools and Colleges, UWL Archives Service, Library staff development and co-manages the development of the Library's resources collection. Prior to joining UWL, she was the Information Specialist for the Science, Engineering and Computing faculty, Kingston University, UK. She is the chair of CILIP's Publicity and Public Relations group. Her professional interests include information literacy, library marketing, inclusive collection development, usability testing, surveys and UX techniques.

Susan Pyzynski has been the Associate Librarian, Technical Services of Houghton Library, Harvard University, USA, since 2005. Prior to coming to Harvard, she was the Librarian for Special Collections and Digital Initiatives at Brandeis University Libraries, USA. Susan currently serves on the operations committee for the Social Networks in Archival Context (SNAC) project administered by the US National Archives and Records Administration. She was an adjunct lecturer at Simmons College, teaching Archival Access and Use in the Masters of Library Science programme, and has spoken frequently on the digitisation of special collections, metadata, library assessment and archival processing.

Tatiana Sanches has a PhD in Education from the University of Lisbon, Portugal; a Master's degree in Education and Reading from the Faculty of Psychology and Educational Sciences; a degree in Modern Languages and Literature (Portuguese Studies) and also a postgraduate degree in Documentation Sciences. She is a researcher in the Unit for Research and Development in Education and Training of the Institute of Education at the University of Lisbon. She also collaborates with the APPsy Unit, ISPA. Currently she is Head of the Documentation Division at the Faculty of Psychology and Institute of Education (University of Lisbon).

Keren Stiles has been undertaking user experience (UX) studies for library systems and projects since 2010, having worked in service development for The Open University's Library Services since 2004. Her role also involves coordination of maintenance and improvements to the library's website and search interface, driven by UX evidence.

Acknowledgements

We are grateful to everyone who has supported us with the writing of this book, whether directly or indirectly. Without the contributions of our case study authors this book would not exist. We are thankful for of the insight they have shared, and their patience over these past few years as we navigated the surprising world of publishing.

From the outset and throughout Linda 'Editor to the Stars' Waterhouse has provided invaluable input and advice. She has not edited this page, so the mistakes are our own. We would also like to acknowledge all at Facet, especially Damian Mitchell for the initial approach.

To the Library Assessment community (our tribe) who have always been so supportive in sharing their knowledge with us – we are forever in your debt. Many of you are present in these pages, whether through direct contributions or referenced work. Too many of you to fully list, but we will always be indebted to Stephen 'The Guvnor' Town for introducing us to each other and for believing in us.

We're thankful to our family and friends for their support. Especially our husbands who have suffered our love of Library Assessment more than anyone else; and our parents who would have been incredibly proud to see our names on a book.

An extra special thanks to Frankie from Selena, for being so utterly awesome and making this fun; and from Frankie to Selena, for being breathtakingly amazing, and without whom not a single word would have been committed to paper.

Chapter 1

Introduction to library assessment

The purpose of this book

Many libraries appreciate the need for assessment, to improve customers' experience, to support advocacy, or both. Librarians reviewing the literature will find no shortage of books to guide them (e.g. Dobbs, 2017; Priestner, 2017; Showers, 2015) and conference papers to inspire them.

The purpose of this book is not to add to the body of knowledge on library assessment, but to address the barriers that most libraries face when considering assessment activities. The central tenet is that there is no need to undertake special data gathering in order to make assessments. Most libraries have huge amounts of data that they have gathered but is sitting on a metaphorical (or in some cases physical) shelf gathering dust, data such as usage statistics, institution-wide survey results, library survey responses and comments books. Using basic skills (all of which can be self-taught from many excellent books within your library and via websites) and a small amount of time, every library can put this data to work to improve customers' experience.

What is library assessment?

Library assessment is the endeavour of determining and communicating how a library is performing, with the aim of driving improvement. There are three key features of library assessment: focus on stakeholders, the goal of improving services to meet stakeholders' needs, and communication of the results and outcomes.

Stakeholders are at the heart of library assessment. They are predominantly library users (and non-users), although assessment extends to determining the performance of the library from the point of view of funders and library staff.

Consequently many library assessment tools and techniques are geared towards learning about the needs of users (and non-users) and evaluating how well the library supports these needs, in order to improve library facilities, services and resources.

Library assessment is not undertaken for the sake of it, or for merely monitoring purposes (for example recording the number of people visiting the library each month). It is measurement for the purpose of improving the programmes and service. Library assessment involves a continuous improvement cycle grounded in customers' expectations – data gathering, analysis, interpretation and contextual-isation, determining implications for the library, acting to effect improvement and reporting, and finally evaluating the changes made.

Communicating the results and outcomes of those results to relevant stakeholders in a meaningful way makes assessment a powerful tool for advocacy. At one end of the scale such communication involves the standard 'closing the loop' of user research, where the results of the survey, interviews or focus groups are communicated back to the population, along with the actions taken to address issues raised. At the other end of the scale it includes using appropriate evidence to support the case being made to funders.

Communicating assessment findings can help to bring stakeholders together. Customers (those using the services) have very different wants and needs from clients (those paying for the services); often they are directly contradictory. Assessment has a unique and valuable role to play in bringing the customer voice to clients, and explaining the position of the clients to customers.

The tools and techniques used cover the whole gamut of those used in the social sciences and statistics. Statistical techniques include descriptive statistics (measures of central tendency and dispersion) and inferential statistics (applying probability theory). They can include quantifying queries raised at the service desk, peak times of library website use, return on investment and library learning analytics. Tools used for statistical analysis range from the ever-dominant Excel and data dashboards through to specialist tools such as SAS Visual Analytics and Tableau.

Social science techniques include surveying, conducting interviews and focus groups, observation, usability testing and user experience research. Where qualitative data is gathered, qualitative data analysis techniques are used to process and interpret it. Data gathering tools range from paper and pen and tape recorders to online survey builders (free or subscribed). Analysis tools include sticky notes, through simple word processing programmes, to specialist qualitative analysis programmes such as NVivo.

Library assessment vs library performance measurement

When deciding the title for this text we debated at length whether we called it 'Putting Library Assessment Data to Work' or 'Putting Library Performance Measurement Data to Work'. As you can tell, we opted for the former.

In 1995, members of the Society of College, National and University Libraries (SCONUL) Advisory Committee on Performance Indicators, supported by the British Library Research and Development Department and Northumbria University, established a biennial conference. The Northumbria International Conference on Performance Measurement and Metrics in Library and Information Services (commonly known as 'Northumbria'; https://libraryperformance.org/) attempted to present a new framework for library measurement. With practitioners and researchers presenting the results of the application of scientific research methodologies to management questions arising from actual situations found in libraries, and keynotes focusing on strategic, political and advocacy questions, Northumbria sought to discuss both the results of performance measurement activities, and also the ideas and forms of performance measurement in libraries.

Over the last 23 years this biennial conference has been held in the USA, South Africa and Italy, although the predominant host of this English language conference has been the UK. It attracts presenters and attendees from around the world, particularly the UK, Europe, North America and Australia. Now known by the somewhat shorter title International Conference on Performance Measurement in Libraries (aka 'LibPMC'), the conference remains the 'invisible college' that connects together those in the field – a field generally referred to because of this link as 'library performance measurement'.

In 2006 Steve Hiller at the University of Washington, Jim Self at the Virginia University, and Martha Kyrillidou at the Association of Research Libraries (ARL) set up the Library Assessment Conference (https://libraryassessment.org/) as a sister conference to LibPMC. The goal of this conference is to build and support a (primarily) North American library assessment community, by bringing together interested practitioners and researchers to stimulate discussion and provide workable ideas for effective, practical and sustainable library assessment.

Despite a long and committed membership of the 'invisible college' of LibPMC, we favour the term 'library assessment' as it avoids the connotation with counting things that the term 'performance measurement' has never quite shaken off.

Why every library needs to undertake assessment

Libraries must serve the same agenda as their 'masters' when demonstrating their quality, impact, value and worth, so those in education, local government and health have faced the same top down pressures as those working in other public sectors. For example, American public libraries are motivated by the same government drives for greater accountability of public money as other public services (Durrance and Fisher-Pettigrew, 2002).

Within the UK library sector, academic libraries have led the way in striving to demonstrate their quality, impact, value and worth. The harsh economic climate of the 1990s pressed higher education institutions for greater accountability and improved attention to quality. In particular, there was the need to demonstrate whether an institution was meeting its goals and objectives, and whether these goals and objectives were aligned with society's needs (Kyrillidou, 1998). Universities were required to account for their performance in teaching and research through research assessment exercises and teaching quality assessments (Town, 1998). In turn, universities began to require accountability and attention to quality from their libraries. The Follett report of 1993 identified libraries as playing a fundamental role in the provision of high-quality education, and in the autumn of that year the sector responded when SCONUL highlighted the quality theme at its conference (Sykes, 1996). However, unlike other public sectors, libraries have their own reasons for wanting to demonstrate their quality. The internet and the increased availability of online services in the 1990s facilitated increasing self-sufficiency for library users. Google and Amazon are real competition for libraries, with unimaginable budgets to spend on providing what their customers want. Libraries could no longer be viewed as storehouses of knowledge where people should want to come because libraries are 'good things' (Stuart and Drake, 1993).

Barriers to library assessment

This book is written by librarians for librarians – whether well established in your career or just starting out via library school. It is for librarians who have library data and know they ought to use it, but experience difficulties under-taking appropriate data gathering exercises, analysing the data, interpreting the results, using the results to make changes, or communicating the outcomes. These difficulties may be due to one or a combination of factors: lack of skills; lack of confidence; lack of time; or lack of money.

The largest barrier to embarking on library assessment is 'paralysis of perfection' – waiting until there is enough time to do it properly; waiting until you feel confident that you have fully mastered all the necessary tools and techniques; waiting until everything is perfect before proceeding. But that point is never reached, and with all that waiting there is no progress. We always advocate that any library assessment activities should be useful and be used. Data collection without action is not only a waste of time but damaging to the reputation of the library. So, if you have collected library data, don't wait for the stars to align – use it. This book will show you how. Your library assessment does not have to be perfect. Good enough is good enough, because any progress towards improving your customers' experiences is better than no progress.

When writing this book we sought case studies from those we knew were using library assessment to great effect. All would (we are sure) admit that their assessment work is not perfect, but all used data to initiate action and so improve the library. Sometimes the action is communicating with customers why you cannot do something they would like because of technical, legal or financial constraints. But action is action: delivering this message effectively is far more beneficial to the library than the perception that you are ignoring customers' concerns, especially if you have canvased their opinion.

Some notes on terminology

Data, information, knowledge

Throughout this book, we use data to cover both quantitative and qualitative items. A piece of data is a value of a characteristic of something. Data is collected and analysed, and as a result of this analysis becomes information suitable for informing decision making. Knowledge is acquired by exposure to many pieces of information about a topic.

Quantitative, qualitative

Quantitative data is objective, quantifiable facts, which are measured and recorded in numbers, for example the number of books you have borrowed from the library this year. This data is numerically focused and can be expressed in graphs, charts and tables. Qualitative data is subjective, and varies depending on the context of its collection, for example how you felt when you read the last book you borrowed from the library. Qualitative data may be expressed in words, pictures, video and numbers, for example asking people to represent their satisfaction with the library service by awarding one, two, three, four or five stars would record this qualitative data numerically.

Impact, value, worth

In a library setting 'impact' is the effect a library has on individuals who interact with it and its services (Markless and Streatfield, 2006). 'Value' is an indication of the importance of a library to its stakeholders and can be defined in a variety of ways, including by use, return on investment, production of a commodity, impact and competing alternatives (Oakleaf, 2010). 'Worth' is the importance of a library to its parent institution or society; it is transcendent – the impact demonstrated must be beyond the library and immediate satisfaction, needs or demands, through contribution to less concrete aspects of institutional or societal intent (Town and Kyrillidou, 2013).

Performance measurement, evaluation

Performance measurement is the process of quantifying the efficiency and effectiveness of past actions in achieving an organisation's goals (Neely, Adams and Kennerley, 2002). There are a number of different performance measurement systems, of which the balanced scorecard (Kaplan and Norton, 1996) is best known. This semi-standard, structured reporting framework covers a small number of financial and non-financial data items, and is used by a management team to track the implementation of a strategy or to monitor operational activities.

Evaluation is the characterisation and appraisal of something's merit. It is undertaken at the end of a significant period of time and is used to judge the impact of a policy, service, programme or activity. Evaluation may compare the results of the appraisal with the original objectives of the policy or service, or may look at what was accomplished and how. The purpose of evaluation is to enable summative reflection in order to inform future decision making.

Metrics, analytics

Metrics are measures of quantitative data. Performance metrics often focus inwardly on the performance of the organisation, but may include performance against customer requirements and value. Performance metrics are linked to corporate strategy and as key performance indicators are often used to measure performance against critical success factors for the organisation (Neely, 2007). Analytics is the discovery, interpretation and communication of meaningful patterns in data, specifically to improve performance.

Analytics is concerned with why what happened in the past happened, and what will happen next (Park, 2017). Analytics makes use of big data and machine learning techniques, mathematics and statistical modelling.

A short history of library assessment

Libraries have been collecting performance measurement data and comparing themselves with others for over 100 years. The Association of College and

Research Libraries (ACRL) has collected statistics since 1907 providing a historic record of the development and trends in library collections and usage in the USA (Thompson, 1951). In Australia, the Council of Australian University Libraries (CAUL) has published its annual statistics since 1953. In contrast, the UK – and Ireland – focused SCONUL statistics were not developed until 1987 (Creaser, 2009).

Initially the focus of measurement was the comparison of inputs (e.g. number of books added to the collection and staffing levels), with the implication being the more money spent, the better the library (Goodall, 1988; Morgan, 1995). The 1985 Jarratt report on university efficiency recommended the development of a range of performance indicators covering input and output measures, for use within the institution and for making comparisons between institutions. The emphasis moved towards cost effectiveness and performance measures relating inputs to outputs (e.g. cost of a loan) as a proxy for quality and impact (Van House, Weil and McClure, 1990). However, measures of inputs, processes and outputs, or composites of these (Cotta-Schonberg, 1995), are not adequate when evaluating, and so demonstrating the quality, impact, value or worth of a library. Such metrics alone cannot determine why a performance gap exists – only the practices on which the metric is based will reveal this (Camp, 1989). The use of performance indicators results in the over-concentration on metrics, because they do not reveal the detail of the processes involved (Town, 1995). Town argued that libraries should be more concerned with performance than measurement, and warned that they were in danger from one of Deeming's seven deadly diseases of western industry: 'management by use only of visible figures, with little or no consideration of figures that are unknown or unknowable' (1998, 83).

Lancour (1951) wrote that libraries should be viewed as progressing through three periods: storehouse, service and 'educational function'. In the 50 years between this statement and the turn of the century, the literature repeatedly celebrated the end of the storehouse period and the move to the service period. However, these were false dawns, with a shift in practice only occurring at the end of this period. During the early 1990s there was a move to mirror this in the performance measures collected: Ford (1989) argued that the only people likely to measure a library's performance by users' needs were the users themselves. Output measures consisting of availability, accessibility and delay were proposed (Thompson, 1991). In addition to output measures, and this user-focused extension of output measures, process data (e.g. processing time for new books) was also included in performance measures (Cotta-Schonberg, 1995).

At the same time, many libraries made the leap to actually asking their users about the quality of the library; a 1995 study found that 81% of UK libraries gathered user feedback (Kinnell and Garrod, 1995). In 1990 the American Library Association had published *Measuring Academic Library Performance: a practical approach*, which provided libraries with a standardised survey tool (Van House, Weil and McClure, 1990), and in 1996 SCONUL launched a standardised survey for libraries to deploy locally (Revill and Ford, 1996). Many university libraries developed their own exit questionnaires for students from general university satisfaction surveys (Lock and Town, 2005).

However, even user satisfaction surveys do not address the issue of performance assessment for quality. Cullen (2001), supported by the work of Nitecki (1996) using SERVQUAL in libraries, proposed that satisfaction with the library service as a whole is more than an aggregate of satisfaction with particular aspects of library provision. Furthermore, when respondents express dissatisfaction in a survey their comments are not helpful because they may only demonstrate that something is wrong, not what is specifically wrong (Whitehall, 1992), or how to fix it, e.g. 'not enough books'.

In the early 2000s, a number of libraries expressed the desire for a survey that would provide information to drive improvements in quality, rather than simply measure customer satisfaction. The ARL partnered with Texas A&M University to develop LibQUAL+ in the USA. Built on the SERVQUAL methodology, the LibQUAL+ research team converted this commercial survey to be suitable for the library sector (Cook, Heath and Thompson, 2002). The key elements of LibQUAL+ are its measurement of minimum, perceived and desired levels of service quality (Lock, 2004). Since its inception over 1350 libraries in 35 countries have used LibQUAL+ (ARL, n.d.).

From the mid-2000s there was also a 'top down' move from government to incorporate user feedback into official information collected about UK academic libraries – the National Student Survey, run annually from 2005, has a question about students' satisfaction with library resources.

Throughout the 2000s there was an increasing focus in the literature on demonstrating the impact of libraries (Poll, 2016). In 2003, a joint project between the Chartered Institute of Information Professionals (CILIP)'s Library and Information Research Group (LIRG) and SCONUL supported 22 UK higher education libraries in developing methods to measure the impact of new initiatives (Payne, 2006). In the USA, the research project Rubric Assessment of Information Literacy Skills (http://railsontrack.info/) funded by the Institute of Museum and Library Services was instigated to help academic librarians and disciplinary faculty assess information literacy outcomes (Holmes and Oakleaf, 2013). Major initiatives in the following decade included the Jisc Library Impact Data Project (Stone and Ramsden, 2013) and the Wollongong University Library Cube (Cox and Jantti, 2012), both of which sought to link library use with student attainment.

Methods for assessing library value began to appear in the literature around 2010, the year when ACRL published *Value of Academic Libraries: a comprehensive research review and report* (Oakleaf, 2010). In the following year the values scorecard was presented at library conferences (Town and Kyrillidou, 2013). In the USA, the three-year LibValue study ran between 2009 and 2012, aiming to define and measure the ways in which the teaching and learning, research, social, professional and public engagement functions of an academic library create value (Mays, Tenopir and Kaufman, 2010).

How to use this book

The previous section may give the impression that every academic library is undertaking broad and deep library assessment activities, and so are continually improving customers' experience and confident in the future funding situation of their library. However, as library assessment practitioners, involved generally in the profession and with LibPMC and Library Assessment Conference, we know that this is not the case.

The literature reflects the work of the enthusiastic few – those at the cutting edge of library assessment. This book is not aimed at them. This book is aimed at librarians who want to improve the experience of their customers but don't know where to start.

The introduction to the topic in each chapter will give you the basics you need to start thinking about how you could apply the methods in your library. We hope the case studies will inspire you, and show how the theory works in the real world. Finally, there are lists of further resources in some chapters with selected items that will enable you to deepen your knowledge.

You can read it cover-to-cover or dip in to specific chapters. The only crucial thing is to have a go yourself – put library data to work in your library and see how recycling existing data can result in improvements for your users.

References

ARL (n.d.) *LibQUAL+: General FAQs*, Association of Research Libraries, https://www.libqual.org/about/about_lq/general_faq.

Camp, R. C. (1989) *Benchmarking: the search for industry best practices that lead to superior performance*, American Society for Quality Control Press.

Cook, C., Heath, F. and Thompson, B. (2002) LibQUAL+: one instrument in the new measures toolbox, *Journal of Library Administration*, **35**, 41–6, doi:10.1300/J111v35n04_09.

Cotta-Schonberg, M. (1995) Performance Measurement in the Context of Quality Management. In Wressell, P. (ed.), *Proceedings of the 1st Northumbria International Conference on Performance Measurement in Libraries and Information Services*, 51–62, Information North.

Cox, B. and Jantti, M. (2012) Discovering the Impact of Library Use and Student Performance, *Educause Review*, July 18, 1–9.

Creaser, C. (2009) UK Higher Education Library Statistics. In Heaney, M. (ed.), *Library Statistics for the Twenty-First Century World*, Walter de Gruyter, 261–72, doi:https://doi.org/10.1515/9783598441677.4.261.

Cullen, R. (2001) Perspectives on User Satisfaction Surveys, *Library Trends*, **49**, 662–86.

Dobbs, A. W. (2017) *The Library Assessment Cookbook*, Association of College and Research Libraries.

Durrance, J. C. and Fisher-Pettigrew, K. E. (2002) Towards Developing Measures of the Impact of Library and Information Services, *Reference & User Services Quarterly*, **42**, 43–53.

Follett, B. (1993) *Joint Funding Councils' Libraries Review Group: Report*, Higher Education Funding Council for England.

Ford, G. (1989) A Perspective on Performance Measurement, *International Journal of Information and Library Research*, **1**, 12–23.

Goodall, D. (1988) Performance Measurement: a historical perspective, *Journal of Librarianship*, **20**, 128–44.

Holmes, C. and Oakleaf, M. (2013) The Official (and Unofficial) Rules for Norming Rubrics Successfully, *Journal of Academic Librarianship*, **39**, 599–602.

Kaplan, R. S. and Norton, D. P. (1996) *The Balanced Scorecard*, Harvard Business School.

Kinnell, M. and Garrod, P. (1995) Benchmarking and its Relevance to the Library and Information Sector. In Wressell, P. (ed.), *Proceedings of the 1st Northumbria International Conference on Performance Measurement in Libraries and Information Services*, 159–71, Information North.

Kyrillidou, M. (1998) *An Overview of Performance Measurement in Higher Education and Libraries*, www.arl.org/newsltr/197/overview.html.

Lancour, H. (1951) Training for Librarianship in North America, *Library Association Record*, September, 280–4.

Lock, S. A. (2004) Update on LibQUAL+ 2004: the international satisfaction survey instrument, *SCONUL Focus*, **31**, 22–3.

Lock, S. A. and Town, J. S. (2005) LibQUAL+ in the UK and Ireland: three years' findings and experience, *SCONUL Focus*, **35**, 41–4.

Markless, S. and Streatfield, D. (2006) *Evaluating the Impact of Your Library*, Facet Publishing.

Mays, R., Tenopir, C. and Kaufman, P. (2010) LibValue: measuring value and return on investment of academic libraries, *Research Library Issues: A Bimonthly Report from ARL, CNI, and SPARC*, **271**, 36–40.

Morgan, S. (1995) *Performance Assessment in Academic Libraries*, Mansell.

Neely, A. D. (2007) *Business Performance Measurement: unifying theory and integrating practice*, 2nd edn, Cambridge University Press.

Neely, A. D., Adams, C. and Kennerley, M. (2002) *The Performance Prism: the scorecard for measuring and managing stakeholder relationships*, Financial Times/Prentice Hall.

Nitecki, D. (1996) Changing the concept and measure of service quality in academic libraries, *Journal of Academic Librarianship*, **22**, 181–90.

Oakleaf, M. (2010) *The Value of Academic Libraries: a comprehensive research review and report*, Association of College and Research Libraries, www.acrl.ala.org/value.

Park, D. (2017) Analysis vs. Analytics: past vs. future, *EE Times*, 26 August, https://www.eetimes.com/author.asp?section_id=36&doc_id=1332172.

Payne, P. (2006) The LIRG/SCONUL Impact Initiative: assessing the impact of HE libraries on learning, teaching, and research, *Library and Information Research*, **30**, 2–12.

Poll, R. (2016) *Bibliography: impacts and outcomes of libraries*, IFLA, https://www.ifla.org/files/assets/e-metrics/bibliography_impact_and_outcome_2016.pdf.

Priestner, A. (ed.) (2017) *User Experience in Libraries: yearbook 2017*, UX in Libraries.

Revill, D. and Ford, G. (1996) *User Satisfaction: standard survey forms for academic libraries*, Society of College, National and University Libraries.

Showers, B. (ed.) (2015) *Library Analytics and Metrics: using data to drive decisions and services*, Facet Publishing.

Stone, G. and Ramsden, B. (2013) Library Impact Data Project: looking for the link between library usage and student attainment, *College and Research Libraries*, **74**, 546–59.

Stuart, C. and Drake, M. A. (1993) TQM in Research Libraries, *Special Libraries*, **84**, 131–6.

Sykes, J. (1996) Quality Issues in Higher Education: the library perspective. In Knowles, B. (ed.), *Routes to Quality: proceedings of the conference held at Bournemouth University 29–31 August 1995*, Bournemouth University Library & Information Services, 1–14.

Thompson, J. (1991) *Redirection in Academic Library Management*, Library Association.

Thompson, L. S. (1951) History of the Measurement of Library Service, *Library Quarterly*, **21** (2), 94–106, doi:10.1086/617755.

Town, J. S. (1995) Benchmarking and Performance Measurement. In Wressell, P. (ed.), *Proceedings of the 1st Northumbria International Conference on Performance Measurement in Libraries and Information Services*, 83–8, Information North.

Town, J. S. (1998) Performance or Measurement? In Wressell, P. (ed.), *Proceedings of the 2nd Northumbria International Conference on Performance Measurement in Libraries and Information Services*, Information North, 81–8.

Town, J. S. and Kyrillidou, M. (2013) Developing a Values Scorecard, *Performance Measurement and Metrics*, **14**, 7–16.

Van House, N. A., Weil, B. T. and McClure, C. R. (1990) *Measuring Academic Library Performance: A Practical Approach*, American Library Association.

Whitehall, T. (1992) Quality in Library and Information Services: a review, *Library Management*, **13**, 23–35.

Chapter 2

Institutional measures of student satisfaction

Chapter overview

Regular surveying of student satisfaction within universities is commonplace. Final year undergraduate students at all UK higher education institutions have completed the National Student Survey (NSS; www.thestudentsurvey.com/) since 2005, which is similar to international surveys. National and international standardised student satisfaction surveys have become more common in the past decade, prior to this the use of surveys to measure student satisfaction was commonly used at a local level. One of the earlier examples of an institutional survey was developed by Student Satisfaction Research Unit at the University of Central England, evaluating the whole university experience, including the Library (Green et al., 1994). General student surveys assessing students' experiences of institutional life vary, depending on the institution setting the questions. Institutional surveys examine a variety of aspects of student life, potentially including teaching and learning, social life, finance, and student support; evaluation of the library is inevitably limited in these forms of assessment. However responses to institutional surveys are often publicised more widely than responses to surveys conducted by libraries so the visibility of these survey results can be greater than for other forms of assessment with senior stakeholders.

In this chapter we explore some of the compulsory and optional standardised methodologies used to measure student satisfaction today, which all have the same common characteristic: a standardised set of questions addressing institution-wide issues. Often institutional-specific issues can be addressed by including questions on local matters. While the library may be assessed when such a standardised methodology is used, it can sometimes be difficult to identify how and where to improve the library based on a single survey question alone. However, there are several advantages of libraries using an institutional survey to gain student feedback about library services:

- the relatively low administration cost to the library as the surveys tend to be administered centrally within the institution
- the use by the institution of modern survey design methods, often resulting in a more comprehensive and robust survey being used
- where standardised surveys are used, being able to benchmark the data, allowing institutions to put their results into context against peer institutions
- when the surveys are compulsory, the response rates are high and results within and outside the institution are usually publicised widely.

Exploiting the methodologies used within your institution could help you to gain insight into your customers' perceptions and your stakeholders' needs. The NSS is widely recognised in the UK. What other institution-wide surveys are being conducted at your institution? Does the survey evaluate your service? If so, how can you exploit its findings to improve your library? If not, how can you encourage the administrators of the survey to do so in future surveys?

The two case studies presented in this chapter show how the NSS has been exploited to improve the library service, and how an institutional survey has been strengthened by including a question asking about the library:

- Case Study 2.1 Use of the National Student Survey to improve library services (Lauren Bjorn, University of Nottingham)
- Case Study 2.2 Collecting low-cost student data through broad collaboration (Zsuzsa Koltay, Cornell University).

In Case Study 2.1 Bjorn shows how you can exploit the data from an institutional standardised survey to inform and lead improvements in the service by analysing the findings for different cohorts. It is a great example of a library using a national survey to effect change at the University of Nottingham.

In Case Study 2.2 Koltay outlines how staff at Cornell University improved a consortium survey through successful lobbying to include questions that ask respondents to evaluate the library service. This collaborative approach has led to improved visibility of the library to senior stakeholders with minimal investment of library staff time.

Compulsory national surveys

The NSS, launched in 2005, provided the first mandated standardised student satisfaction survey for UK higher education institutions. The survey is typically sent to final year undergraduate students in England, Northern Ireland, Scotland and Wales on behalf of the respective funding bodies. Consisting of 27 standardised questions and an open text comments box, the survey contains one question evaluating student satisfaction with the library. From 2005 until 2016 the wording of the question was 'The library resources and services are good enough for my needs'. In 2017 this was amended to 'The library resources (e.g. books, online services and learning spaces) have supported my learning well' (HEFCE, 2016). The results of the NSS are published on the Unistats website (https://unistats.direct.gov.uk/), enabling prospective students to compare institutions and courses.

As a result of the survey, senior university administrators have placed increased importance on student satisfaction. Research conducted by Stanley (2009) found the introduction of the NSS had led to institutions developing action plans, monitored by senior executives, to improve satisfaction. Library directors reported that good scores resulted in institutional esteem, while bad scores helped increase institutional investment in the library (Stanley, 2009). It is not coincidental that a series of capital investment projects in library space development started shortly after the launch of the NSS. In the initial years after the launch, library directors reported that receiving either high or low scores worked in the library's favour, whereas libraries in the middle of the table were overlooked as they were not viewed to be problem or a success to be celebrated.

How can you exploit the data gathered through the NSS to improve your library? Having only one standardised question and unstructured free-text comment could be viewed as having limited value. It is not possible to focus the question on specific areas of concern or to glean feedback on local strategic issues. However, the NSS provides a large amount of information from final year undergraduates, with an overall response rate of 72% (HEFCE, 2017). The insights gained can provide indicators of where there are opportunities for improvement within the service.

In Case Study 2.1 Bjorn shows how effective data analysis at different organisational levels can identify differences in satisfaction, leading to refocusing of resources to target areas of dissatisfaction. Combining qualitative and quantitative results to gain further insight has helped the University of Nottingham identify where it can make improvements. The NSS provides an opportunity to reduce primary research time by exploiting qualitative data effectively to identify areas where further focused research may be necessary.

The Australian Equivalent to the NSS is the Student Experience Survey, which is distributed to all first-year and last-year students (Social Research Centre, n.d.). Respondents to the Student Experience Survey are asked to rate the following seven aspects of learning resources provided by their course:

- teaching spaces (e.g. lecture theatres, tutorial rooms, laboratories)
- student spaces and common areas
- online learning materials
- computing and IT resources
- assigned books, notes and resources
- laboratory or studio equipment
- library resources and facilities.

As with the NSS, the scores are publicly available and comparable between institutions, leading institutional administrators to place increased importance on the scores.

Optional institutional surveys

In addition to, or in some cases instead of, national student satisfaction surveys, some institutions choose to evaluate satisfaction using different methodologies.

I-graduate (www.i-graduate.org) provides global benchmarks for students' experience. Its International Student Barometer (https://www.i-graduate.org/services/international-student-barometer/) is an opt-in service that evaluates the perceptions of international students at higher education institutions. Its sister product, the Student Barometer (https://www.i-graduate.org/services/student-barometer/), assesses perceptions of international and domestic students using the same methodology, for example there are questions asking respondents to rate the 'online library' and the 'physical library'. Results are benchmarked against competitor groups and national and international indices.

Within the UK, i-graduate has partnered with the Higher Education Academy to administer the postgraduate equivalent of the NSS. The Postgraduate Taught Experience Survey (PTES) is distributed to taught postgraduates, and the Postgraduate Research Experience Survey (PRES) is distributed to research students. Both surveys contain a single statement on the library and ask whether respondents agree with it; the wording is slightly different in each methodology:

- PTES: 'the library resources and services are good enough for my needs (including physical and online)'
- PRES: 'there is adequate provision of library facilities (including physical and online resources)'.

Survey data can be benchmarked but, unlike with the NSS, running the survey at a university is not compulsory and the survey data is not published at individual institutional level (Higher Education Academy, 2015).

In the USA, all states regulate higher education differently (Kelly, James and Rooney, 2015), and there is no demand for federal compulsory assessment of student satisfaction. Methodologies tend to operate at sector or institution level rather than at a state or federal level. However, there are some optional national tools. The Cooperative Institutional Research Program survey, administered by the Higher Education Research Institute (https://heri.ucla.edu/), assesses students' satisfaction with the library and how frequently they use library resources. The National Survey on Student Engagement (http://nsse.indiana.edu/) is designed to assess the extent to which students engage in educational practices associated with high levels of learning and development. Interestingly this extensive survey does not assess students' engagement with library content, services or skills development.

In Case Study 2.2 Koltay describes how the Consortium on Financing Higher Education (COFHE; http://web.mit.edu/cofhe/) Enrolled Student Survey was improved by including questions on library provision. This ultimately led to an improved library service and student experience at Cornell University thanks to the data insight gained.

Case Study 2.1   Use of the National Student Survey to improve library services at the University of Nottingham
Lauren Bjorn

Introduction
Libraries, Research and Learning Resources (LRLR) is a professional service department at the University of Nottingham. Our eight UK libraries serve a community of over 33,000 students and 7000 staff with a comprehensive range of services. The libraries have 1.3 million print books and journals, 0.5 million e-books and subscriptions to nearly 43,000 e-journals, 3.5 million manuscripts including special collections of international importance, and a full range of learning technologies.

In recent years, LRLR has embraced a data-driven, evidence-based approach to the development and enhancement of the wide range of services we offer. This case study describes the approach we have taken to analysing and maximising the impact of our NSS results. The case study discusses the motivation for a new approach, describes the method we developed, and explores the impact it has had and the challenges we have faced along the way.

Untapped opportunities

The higher education environment is rapidly changing. The University of Nottingham's Global Strategy 2020 explains that 'Changing student expectations, the globalisation of higher education, disruptive new technologies and increased competition for the best talent means we must regularly review our goals and actions if we are to achieve long-term success' (University of Nottingham, 2015).

Core to achieving this, the university and the library must enhance the student experience. At Nottingham we are committed to putting students at the heart of everything we do. Our success in this hinges on our ability to listen to our students, to understand their frustrations and the challenges they face, and build on this knowledge by:

- making tangible improvements to the way we do things
- improving and targeting communications to raise awareness of our services
- giving honest explanations of why we do things the way we do.

Surveys are increasingly important to understanding student opinion and experience. Academic schools and professional service departments alike are vying for our students' attention; we all want to know what students like and don't like about our own particular offering. But how can we understand our students' experience of their libraries, and respond to these in an agile and timely manner, without contributing to the ever-growing problem of over-surveying and survey fatigue? Furthermore, how can we empower and enable all LRLR staff, not just those in senior or strategic positions, to understand the student experience? And how can we ensure that all LRLR staff are aware of the role they play in addressing student concerns? Our answer? To make more of the rich information that students already provide in their responses to national standardised surveys by comprehensively analysing and visualising the data, and making it available to all staff in ways that are easy to engage with.

Each year approximately 70% of our final year undergraduates complete the NSS. In 2016, 63% of University of Nottingham NSS respondents left an open text comment, but the library did not make maximum use of the subtle insights of the quantitative data, nor the more specific insights of the nuanced qualitative data these comments provided. Previously our use of this data has been limited to making basic calculations of student satisfaction and relatively inconsistent and ad hoc use of open text comments. There were not enough staff who were 'data literate' and had the time to devote to making more complex analyses.

Students tell us that while they see the value in contributing to surveys, they want to see how their feedback influences tangible change. If we do not use the information provided in the NSS data and open text comments, and evidence this through change and/or communication, there is a risk that we will inadvertently contribute to student dissatisfaction. To maximise our use of the data, inform tangible change and improve student satisfaction, we have developed a new analytical framework, which ensures we get as great a return as possible on the investment of time and effort students make in completing the NSS.

A new analytical framework

The framework has four core elements:

- a calculation of student satisfaction at different organisational levels, from institution to individual academic school
- satisfaction thresholds to identify academic schools where interventions or further exploration may be required
- consistent coding of the open text comments to library features and sub-features using a departmentally agreed 'codebook' and the qualitative analysis software NVivo
- interactive presentation of the data and analyses in a Tableau dashboard, enabling all staff to ask and answer questions using the data from strategic perspectives, e.g. key performance indicators (KPIs), to operational perspectives.

A key feature of the framework is the comprehensive, consistent and repeatable nature of the analysis, which allows for robust, longitudinal investigations of the data. The framework also makes it easy to use the NSS data to create plans of prioritised, trackable actions, and then communicate decisions back to students to close the feedback loop.
   The action plan is divided into three sections:

- *quick wins and 'wish I'd knowns'* open text comments that identify quick and easy improvements that can be made to the existing library service, or existing services that students wish they had known about sooner or seem to have never found out about in the first place
- *suggestions*: open text comments suggesting additions to our services
- *opportunities for improvement:* using a combination of open text comments and quantitative data to identify opportunities for improvement that apply across all faculties and libraries, or are specific to a faculty or school, or to one of our eight libraries.

The NSS Tableau dashboard

Interactive visualisations allow all LRLR staff to generate and answer their own questions about the NSS data. These questions could reflect the strategic priorities of the department and wider university, such as achieving certain satisfaction levels, or may be more nuanced questions relating to aspects of an individual staff member's role. For example, our librarians who work directly with faculties might want to explore satisfaction and comments within certain academic schools, whereas our collections librarians might use the open text comments to support or inform purchasing decisions.

Designing a dashboard to meet such a range of possible needs is challenging and only achievable if designed collaboratively with users. We wanted to find out how satisfied students at the university are by asking:

- How satisfied are students with different aspects of their university experience (e.g. feedback, assessment, teaching), and how have these satisfaction levels changed over recent years? (see Figure 2.1)
- How does satisfaction with the libraries compare with other aspects of the university experience?
- How satisfied are students with our library facilities? Are we meeting our KPI targets?
- Is the overall institutional picture hiding notable trends in library satisfaction at the faculty or school level?

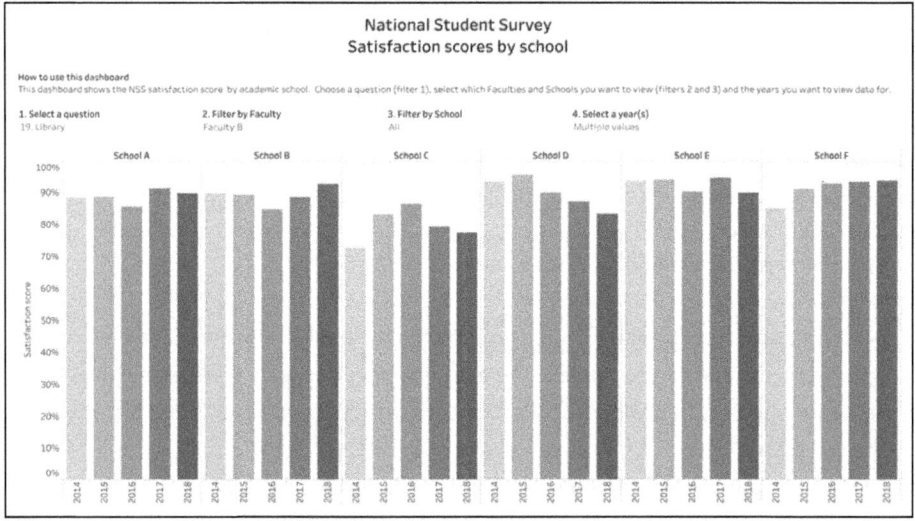

Figure 2.1 *Screenshot from the LRLR NSS Tableau dashboard showing trends in users' satisfaction rates with the library by school, 2012–16*

We wanted to know how our student satisfaction levels compare with other institutions:

- How does student satisfaction with University of Nottingham libraries compare with student satisfaction levels at competitor institutions, including our benchmarking group?

- How does this vary for our different faculties and schools? This analysis assumes that other institutions have a similar academic school structure to ours.
- What trends in library satisfaction can we see in our benchmarking group? Are there any opportunities for sharing best practice?

We wanted to know what the open text comments are telling us:

- What proportion of students made comments (positive or negative) about the library (see Figure 2.2)?
- Which features of the library appear to be most important to our students (were mentioned most frequently)?
- Where could we make improvements to the student experience of our libraries (which aspects of the library received the greatest proportion of dissatisfied comments)?
- Are there any faculty- or school-specific concerns?
- Are there any concerns specific to one of our eight libraries?
- What evidence do we have to support changes in, or extensions to, our service offering?

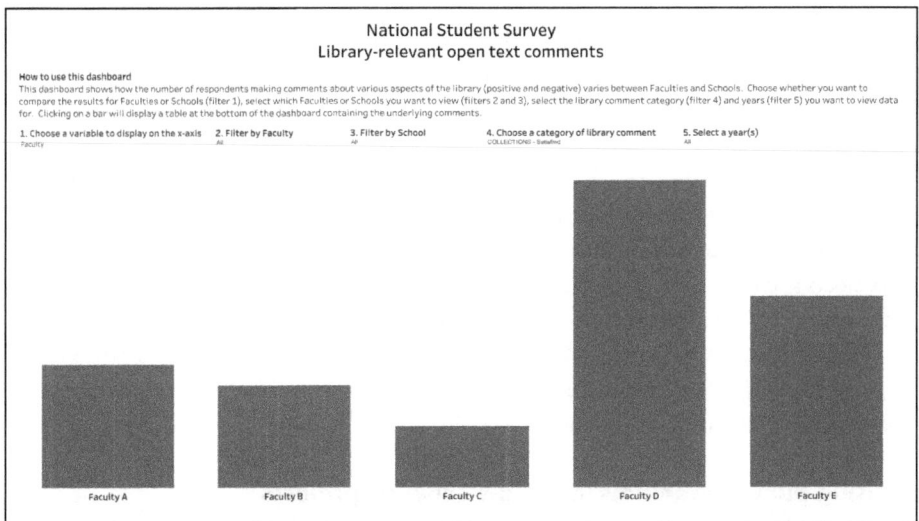

Figure 2.2 *Screenshot from the LRLR NSS Tableau dashboard showing the distribution of positive comments about our collections for different faculties.*
The dashboard can display the comments underlying the individual bars, but these are not shown to protect student anonymity.

These are some comments on the impact of using the framework:

As someone who was new to HE [higher education], libraries, the university, the department [LRLR], Tableau etc., the NSS data being presented in an accessible and easily digestible way massively improved my efficiency and quickly got me up to speed on the impact of the department.

LRLR colleague

The department has built an excellent reputation across the university for its engagement with students. The framework has given us the ability to be systematic, targeted and impactful in that engagement.

Director of LRLR

Helping students get the books they need when they need them

There have been several significant benefits of using the framework. It has been instrumental in allowing us to use evidence to target specific areas of low satisfaction. Before the framework, we knew that students had concerns about finding the right books and journals in the right format at the right time, but we had no idea which subject areas were most affected. The framework has provided a mechanism by which we can find out which they are, and has consequently revolutionised the way we prioritise our efforts.

Being able to drill down into the quantitative and qualitative information at school level (Figure 2.1) has allowed us and our academic partners to understand the student experience at a more granular level. For example, this has informed our focusing of resources and efforts to increase online reading list uptake to specific academic areas. It has also informed the creation of a new communication campaign to make it easier for students to ask us to buy additional copies of books, and to request additions to our stock and interlibrary loans.

The ability to visualise comments by school and/or subject (Figure 2.2) quickly has allowed us to have more constructive and efficient meetings with academic and professional service partners. We have used the framework to inform a number of student-led projects such as 'Students as Change Agents' (www.nottingham.ac.uk/currentstudents/ studentopportunities/students-as-change-agents/index.aspx), which aims to improve students' access to, and understanding of, library resources. In addition, the framework has supported the case for changing book budget allocations so they better balance the needs of research and undergraduate studies.

Focusing our requirements in complex change projects

Students are key stakeholders in all complex change projects. The framework makes it easy to incorporate student opinion at the project initiation stage. For example, staff running a project attempting to change our resource discovery tool were able to use the NSS dashboard to understand students' frustrations with our existing provision and translate these into service requirements. Alongside other consultations this has reduced our need to collate baseline data through surveys or focus groups and instead allowed us to focus our student interactions on more in-depth, informative questions about specific system functionality.

Strategic perspectives

From a strategic perspective, the dashboard allows us easily and quickly to display evidence to support investment bids and demonstrate value. For example, Nottingham's recent Teaching Excellence Framework submission references the rise in student satisfaction with library services (University of Nottingham, 2017). We have been able to generate data and visualisations on the propensity for students to express dissatisfaction with aspects of the library space in order to make the case for investing in library buildings.

Challenges and recommendations when using this approach

Once a person is familiar with the tools, it is technically easy to make a dashboard, but it is harder to make meaningful dashboards that people can understand at a glance and feel comfortable using. Data can be scary to the uninitiated. People's fear of 'breaking' the dashboard, of misinterpreting the results, or of assuming that they won't understand what they are seeing can be enough to prevent them from using the tool in the first place. Providing 'safe environments' where staff can interact with the dashboard under supervision is important to develop their confidence.

Getting the design of the dashboard right is just as important as planning its roll-out and uptake. No matter how many training sessions you run, you want colleagues to be able to use and understand the data independently. Our experience to date has informed the following best practice tips:

- *Keep it visual*, with only the necessary explanatory text. Dashboards are meant to be simple and easy to understand; graphs are usually much easier to 'read' than text and tables. Have an accompanying glossary if you think colleagues would appreciate extra guidance.
- *Keep it simple*. Don't overcomplicate your visuals with 3D effects, lots of colours and font styles, or unusual graph types. Let people get straight to the information as easily as possible.
- *Have a consistent style*, for example, use the same types of filters and put them in the same place on every dashboard.
- *Do some research and involve your colleagues in the dashboard design*. What kind of questions do your colleagues want to ask of the data? What kind of views do you need to produce? What filters will enable your colleagues to drill down to the information they are interested in?
- *Provide use cases*. Instead of providing purely operational instructions on how to interact with the dashboard, incorporate instructions into example use cases taking users through some of the questions they can explore on the dashboard. This approach will familiarise users with the dashboard mechanics and help them appreciate and understand how the dashboard can become a proactive tool.

- *Be mindful of data protection.* To preserve student anonymity the open text comments should not be used in any publicly available materials; other members of your institution may have sensitivities about how the open text comments are shared and used internally.

Summary

Simple satisfaction scores based on one question about the library can tell us only so much. The framework represents a step-change from obtaining broad insights from basic calculations of student satisfaction to a unique position where all staff can have a detailed understanding of how our libraries are performing within the wider higher education sector. Working alongside our department's Communication and Engagement Team, and the internal University Marketing and Communications Department, the framework also informs library staff in making a structured approach in response to students' suggestions and therefore closing the feedback loop.

We will continue to evolve the analytical framework to meet the changing needs of our colleagues. This will empower everyone to own their personal contributions to improving the student experience allowing us to embed the students views at the heart of everything we do.

Case Study 2.2 Collecting low-cost student data through broad collaboration at Cornell University
Zsuzsa Koltay

Summary

This case study focuses on a broad collaboration between libraries, institutional research staff and the Consortium on Financing Higher Education (COFHE) – a project that resulted in a block of library questions on the Consortium's Enrolled Student Survey. There were 27 participating institutions, whose staff chose to run the same library question in the first year, resulting in directly comparable student experience data with low or no overhead for these libraries. The responses to one of the COFHE questions showed that students assigned a lower than hoped for rating when asked how useful they thought library instruction was. At Cornell University Library these findings resulted in a pilot project to create instructional videos and, through another collaboration, build them into the active learning redesign of two engineering courses. The pilot's success led to a library-wide programme of instructional video creation, thereby refocusing information literacy instruction.

The problem

As evidence-based decision making has become universally supported and practised in higher education, including in academic libraries, some drawbacks of collecting the needed data have become apparent. Survey fatigue, in particular, has become a widespread issue and has resulted in plunging response rates as more and more survey instruments are fielded by more and more units of our complex organisations. The desire to improve student experience is admirable, but if students are asked to complete too many surveys they can become disillusioned, which can have a detrimental effect on the validity of the data collected. Also, creating a well-designed survey to produce actionable data is not a trivial task; it requires a specific skill set and can take a lot of time and effort.

The solution

Collaboration to reduce the number of surveys aimed at students while still collecting useful data for multiple stakeholders is one logical solution to this problem and has the added benefit of lowering the overhead required to get the data the library needs to align its services with students' needs.

Most US colleges and universities charge their central institutional research departments with understanding and charting trends in the student experience. In many cases this goal is accomplished via a system of census surveys conducted on a predictable schedule. For example, incoming first-year students might be surveyed every year, all seniors in even years, and all enrolled undergraduates in odd years. Staff in higher educational institutions often choose to conduct such surveys as part of a consortium so they can evaluate their findings against those of normative peer groups. Other benefits of consortium-initiated surveys include a shared, thoughtful and thorough survey design process that balances consortium-wide and local needs by having a shared survey core and centrally offered optional question modules, and a chance to add local-only questions.

Cornell University is part of the COFHE, a group of 35 highly selective private universities and colleges of varying sizes. The COFHE provides its members with a suite of surveys designed to probe the experience of their undergraduate student bodies. COFHE staff and committees create the instruments while the institutional research staff of each member decide whether and when to participate and select optional questions to add to the core ones as well as local questions based on stakeholders' needs at their specific institutions.

The collaboration

Cornell University Library has worked with Cornell's Institutional Research and Planning Department for years to include local questions about the library on these surveys. For example, starting in 2010 the senior survey participants have been asked to rate the library's contribution to their academic success, their efficiency, their ability to do research, and their ability to evaluate information sources critically. The results are mostly used for communication purposes in order to demonstrate the value that the library brings to students.

In 2015 the COFHE was getting ready to run its survey of all undergraduate students when the idea arose at Cornell to try to place library questions in the shared part of the survey rather than the local one. From such an approach we hoped:

- to add the ability to benchmark the responses across the libraries of many institutions
- to maximise responses for the library; from that year on local questions would have had to be placed at the very end of the instrument, out of the natural flow of questions, thus risking receiving significantly lower response rates.

Given the fairly limited window of opportunity we had to place library questions on the survey, the entire collaborative process was conducted via e-mail with the following major steps:

- Assemble a small group of librarians representing a few COFHE institutions. Using assessment listservs and existing professional contacts, a handful of librarians discussed shared assessment needs that could be met through COFHE survey questions. Most of the discussion centred on self-reported impact (along the lines of the above-cited local questions on Cornell's senior survey) and on probing the usefulness of various library offerings. The group agreed to advocate with COFHE for shared library questions.
- Approach COFHE with our needs and desire to have library questions asked across institutions. Staff at COFHE were very receptive to the idea and suggested we offer an optional library module to the members of the consortium. COFHE staff and local contacts at the Institutional Research and Planning Department were helpful in suggesting possible formulations and placements on the questionnaire to fit in with the existing core of the instrument.
- Finalise the module through further discussions with librarians and COFHE. This step resulted in a module that our COFHE partners could agree to and share with the institutions that were getting ready to run the survey.
- Reach out to librarians at COFHE institutions about to run the survey. Since the decision about what questions to include rested with each institution's institutional research staff, it was important to contact librarians across the consortium to bring their attention to the availability of these questions and to encourage them to lobby to include the new module. We received a lot of positive reactions from our library colleagues who were happy to have the new option available to them. Some already had working relationships with their institutional research colleagues, but several others communicated with them for the first time through their involvement with this project. Some had not been aware of the COFHE surveys at all.
- Co-ordinate question selection. COFHE provided us with real-time feedback on which institutions were adding which questions. We also heard from some librarians as their institutions were weighing the options and they were building relationships with their institutional research colleagues. This step allowed us an opportunity to co-ordinate what questions different institutions chose so that as many of the libraries as possible would have directly comparable results.

- Share outcomes. Once the survey was run and the results were available, librarians shared the results and discussed next steps via e-mail.

The new module

The new module, situated in the section of the survey that probed students' experience of obtaining advice at the university, allowed institutions to choose one of two possible questions:

- whether students used the library (including study space, services, electronic and print resources), and if so how helpful they found it to be; this option added only one question to the instrument – a big advantage for those whose surveys were already too long – but responses did not provide granular information about different aspects of the library, so there were limitations in interpreting the results and in using them to determine what follow-up steps were necessary
- asking separately about the use and usefulness of study spaces, research help, electronic and print resources, and library classes and presentations; the questions and the possible answer categories (not very helpful, somewhat helpful, very helpful, have not used) fitted in with the rest of the survey instrument.

Out of the colleges and universities that ran the Enrolled Student Survey that year, we were pleased that 29 included one of these library-related questions, 27 of which used the second option in order to obtain directly comparable and more granular results. Our outreach to librarians and their advocacy with their institutional research units obviously paid off.

The findings

Cornell University Library's findings from the survey were shared with the library with a comparison to two normative groups. This presentation echoed that of the findings of the full survey and was based on the Institutional Research and Planning Department's definition of Cornell's peer groups. There was an overall response rate of 36% as 4892 Cornell students completed the survey.

The results showed that the features of the library undergraduate students used most widely were study space, followed by electronic and print resources, research help, and library classes and presentations. Although Cornell students used the library services more than students in the normative groups, the relative ranking of these four aspects of library services was the same for all the participating institutions. Usefulness levels assigned by the students at Cornell followed the same ranking as those assigned by students in the two normative groups, with study space being considered the most useful and library classes and presentations the least useful, and there was little difference in rankings between students in the normative groups and Cornell students.

The impact

In discussing the results, Cornell University Library staff were most interested in improving the lowest ranked service: library classes and presentations. Through a partnership with one of the colleges, subject librarians redesigned two courses as a pilot and reconceived library presentations as a series of short videos integrated into Blackboard to support students undertaking specific assignments requiring the necessary research skills. Students could watch these videos as needed at just the right time in the semester, at the point of need. They could speed up or slow down the videos, skip them altogether or review them multiple times depending on their individual needs. Use data showed that the videos were watched most heavily just before the particular assignments were due, but that they were also reviewed later in the semester. The subject librarians featured in the videos received positive e-mail feedback on this approach and further reference enquiries. This showed us that the videos helped maintain the face recognition and personal contact that traditional presentations achieve. A mid-semester course evaluation conducted by the college showed that 72% of the students preferred the video approach to the traditional class presentations, 17% had no preference, and only 11% would have preferred presentations.

Because of the success of the pilot, which was conceived in direct response to the COFHE survey results, a task force was formed at Cornell University Library charged with creating the infrastructure and support structure for producing and using instructional videos on a wider scale. Thus, the low-cost data generated by our collaboration with the Institutional Research and Planning Department and COFHE has engendered a shift in how information literacy instruction is going to be delivered at Cornell. We hope to trace the impact of this change on students' perception at the next administration of the COFHE survey.

Conclusions

Collaborating with campus institutional research staff and applicable consortia to place library-specific questions on student experience surveys proved to be an effective approach for the library. As this case study shows, such collaboration can result in useful, actionable data and a benchmarking comparison with minimal investment of library staff time and without creating more survey fatigue. As these questions are asked on an instrument that produces data that many campus stakeholders and decision makers pay attention to, the findings get more visibility than most other library data.

Acknowledgements

The author would like to acknowledge the following colleagues for their roles in making it possible to add the library question module to the COFHE Enrolled Student Survey: Steve Minicucci, Director of Research for the Consortium on Financing Higher Education; Marne K. Einarson, Assistant Director of Institutional Research and Planning, Cornell University; Nisa Bakkalbasi, Assessment Coordinator, Columbia University Libraries; Lisa R. Horowitz,

Assessment Librarian/Linguistics Librarian, MIT Libraries; Mary Ann Mavrinac, Vice Provost, and Andrew H. and Janet Dayton Neilly Dean, River Campus Libraries, University of Rochester; and Sarah Tudesco, Assessment Librarian, Yale University Library.

Conclusions

The two case studies in the chapter demonstrate how institutional measures of student satisfaction can be used effectively to improve library services. While these methodologies have been criticised for lacking specificity to enable service improvements, they have been noticed by senior administrators and cannot be ignored. At the University of Nottingham and Cornell University the data has been successfully exploited to improve the student experience.

Identifying the surveys being used by your institution is a vital step in this process, even if they currently do not assess the library. As Koltay demonstrated, it is possible to improve institutional surveys, even at a consortium level, by including library assessment. Working collaboratively with colleagues in institutional research departments, other librarians and consortium contacts can benefit everyone. The benchmarkable nature of these standardised instruments is their key strength, allowing you to identify the strengths within your service and opportunities for improvement.

References

Green, D., Brannigan, C., Mazelan, P. and Giles, L. (1994) Measuring Student Satisfaction: a method of improving the quality of the student experience? In Haselgrove, S. (ed.), *The Student Experience,* 100–7, The Society for Research into Higher Education & Open University Press.

Higher Education Academy (2015) *Higher Education Academy Student Surveys,* https://www.heacademy.ac.uk/institutions/surveys.

HEFCE (2016) *A New National Student Survey for 2017,* Higher Education Funding Council for England, www.hefce.ac.uk/pubs/Year/2016/CL,302016/.

HEFCE (2017) *National Student Survey,* Higher Education Funding Council for England, www.hefce.ac.uk/lt/nss/.

Kelly, A. P., James, K. J. and Rooney, C. (2015) Inputs, Outcomes, Quality Assurance: a closer look at state oversight of higher education, American Enterprise Institute, https://www.aei.org/wp-content/uploads/2015/08/Inputs-Outcomes-Quality-Assurance.pdf.

Social Research Centre (n.d.) QILT – Quality Indicators for Learning and Teaching, https://www.qilt.edu.au/.

Stanley, T. (2009) The National Student Survey: Pain or Gain?, *SCONUL Focus*, **45**, 144–7, www.sconul.ac.uk/publications/newsletter/.

University of Nottingham (2015) *Global Strategy 2020*, www.nottingham.ac.uk/about/documents/uon-global-strategy-2020.pdf.

University of Nottingham (2017) *Application to the Teaching Excellence Framework 2017*, www.nottingham.ac.uk/about/documents/tef/tef-feb2017.pdf.

Chapter 3

Standardised library surveys

Chapter overview

In this chapter we explore some of the more common standardised library survey methodologies, and share case studies from three libraries whose staff have used these forms of assessment. Standardised library surveys, commonly developed by national library associations or commercial providers, focus on assessing customers' perceptions of the library service in a consistent manner. These surveys have enabled library staff to assess their users' requirements and satisfaction levels with limited development costs; their key strength is the ability to compare performance against sector averages and/or other libraries using the same methodology.

Typically the questions evaluate common aspects of library provision at a broad level, for example by asking respondents about their perceptions of library information provision. Library staff choose this methodology if they wish to compare their service with other libraries where similar surveys are used, or as an aggregated data set thereof. They may also choose a standardised tool if they wish to evaluate the library services at a general, broad level without going to the expense of developing a bespoke local survey. Users of standardised tools typically repeat the methodology over a period of time to assess the impact any changes have had and to monitor customers' perceptions longitudinally. Standardised library surveys cannot evaluate local issues, for example perceptions of a unique or uncommon service.

Standardised library surveys are a long-established form of assessment. In 1990 the American Library Association published *Measuring Academic Library Performance: a practical approach*, providing libraries with a standardised survey tool (Van House, Weil and McClure, 1990). Previous assessment activity had focused on quantitative measures of library expenditure and operational activity. Van House, Weil and McClure sought to address the gap in assessing user experience of libraries. They provided different survey tools in the book, including a general satisfaction survey and one focusing on material availability, tabulation forms for survey analysis and examples of data presentation.

In the UK the Society of College, National and University Libraries (SCONUL) launched a standardised survey for libraries to deploy locally in 1996 (Revill and Ford, 1996). This briefing paper provided academic libraries with questions they were free to adapt to local circumstances, but reduced the time needed for a library to create a survey themselves. This work was revised in 2004 when a refreshed survey was developed (West, 2004). Although the questions are standardised, administration and analysis of the survey is managed as an in-house survey would be. The flexibility of the survey and local management of the data has proven to be a barrier to benchmarking (Creaser, 2006).

Around the turn of the millennium, as the internet was used more often as an everyday business tool, online surveys were deployed and analysed electronically. The amount of literature on standardised survey tools in library assessment increased, with LibQUAL+ (https://www.libqual.org) and the Rodski survey (now known as the Insync survey) being made available for libraries to use at their institutions. Similarly, Ithaka S+R launched a survey of the perceptions of US faculty at the same time, which formed the basis of the local survey it provides today.

The Association of Research Libraries (ARL) partnered with Texas A&M Libraries to develop LibQUAL+ in the USA. Built on the SERVQUAL methodology, the LibQUAL+ research team converted this commercial survey to be suitable for the library sector (Cook, Heath and Thompson, 2002). This assessment tool is discussed in more detail below, supported by Case Study 3.1 from the University of Limerick.

Around the same time as LibQUAL+ was being developed in the USA, staff in a group of Australasian libraries were conducting similar research adapting the SERVQUAL methodology to the library sector (Trahn et al., 2001). This research formed the basis of the Rodski survey tool, subsequently known as the Insync survey, which is commonly used by Australian University Libraries. Case Study 3.2 from the University of Sydney discusses how this has been used to assess and improve the library service.

The Ithaka S+R surveys differed slightly in that they are not based on the SERVQUAL methodology. Ithaka S+R, the research branch of Ithaka, which also operates the JSTOR and ARTSTOR services, developed a regular survey of faculty's views of scholarly communications and information usage. This triannual survey has been used since 2000 in the USA. Results are aggregated and reported on at a national level, providing insight into trends within the sector, for example the US faculty survey 2015 (Wolff, Rod and Schonfeld, 2016a), and the UK version conducted in partnership with Jisc and Research Libraries UK (Wolff, Rod and Schonfeld, 2016b). In 2014 the surveys were expanded to include additional customer groups, and a new local survey service was developed to allow libraries to use the same questions in a local setting. In Case Study 3.3 Hoffman discusses how this methodology has been used by undergraduates, graduates and faculty members at the University of Nevada, Las Vegas (UNLV).

The following case studies are presented in this chapter:

- Case Study 3.1 LibQUAL+ as a catalyst for change at the University of Limerick (Ciara McCaffrey and Michelle Breen, University of Limerick)
- Case Study 3.2 The Insync survey at the University of Sydney (Belinda Norman, University of Sydney)
- Case Study 3.3 Ithaka S+R local surveys at the UNLV Libraries (Starr Hoffman, University of Nevada).

LibQUAL+

The LibQUAL+ survey, provided by the Association of Research Libraries (ARL), is a standardised methodology for measuring customers' perceptions and expectations of the library, asking 22 questions to evaluate the library in three aspects of service: premises (library as place), content (information control) and staff (affect of service). The web-based survey is customised by the local library with personalised demographics (e.g. subject disciplines, branch library details), logos and contact details. The library staff can add five additional questions to the survey should they wish to. It can be completed by undergraduates, postgraduate/graduate students, academic and faculty staff, library staff and other staff, depending on who the library staff wish to survey. When ready, library staff are responsible for distributing the survey to their sample or target population.

The survey uses gap theory, adapted from the SERVQUAL methodology (Cook and Heath, 2001). For each core question respondents are asked to rate the item on three separate nine-point scales covering their minimum service level, their desired service level and their perception of current provision. These scores are then used to calculate an adequacy score (the gap between minimum and perceived scores), a superiority score (the gap between the perceived and the desired scores) and a zone of tolerance (the range between the minimum and desired scores). The target is for the perception of the item being evaluated to fall somewhere within the zone of tolerance, with an aim to increase perceptions so they meet the desired level of service. Should perceptions fail to meet minimum expectations (indicated by a negative adequacy score) these items are identified as key priorities for improvement. Should the library find it is exceeding customers' expectations in some areas (shown through a positive superiority score) managers may realign resource and staff time to support areas where improvements need to be made.

Initial analysis of the survey data is provided by LibQUAL+, with all participants receiving a results notebook containing their scores broken down by the key users groups: overall scores, undergraduates, postgraduate and graduate, academic and faculty, library staff and other (depending on their sample). Participants get access to all results from all fellow participants for the year(s) they participated so they can benchmark their scores against them; they may also receive a consortium notebook containing the aggregated results of libraries within their peer group. Along with their own institutional notebooks (and a consortium notebook if applicable), participants also receive the raw data of their survey responses for further detailed analysis, and real-time access to the qualitative feedback received.

LibQUAL+ offers libraries a relatively affordable, easy to administer, standardised survey tool, which allows benchmarking between participating institutions. It has been used successfully to improve over 1300 libraries in 35 countries, an example of which is described in Case Study 3.1 from the University of Limerick in Ireland.

Insync

Similar to LibQUAL+, the Insync survey (http://educationandlibraries. insyncsurveys.com.au/our-services/library-client-survey/, previously known as the Rodski survey) uses gap theory to assess respondents' perceptions of the library on a seven-point scale. There are 28 statements for respondents to consider, in five categories: communication, service delivery, facilities and equipment, library staff and information resources. Respondents are asked to rate each statement on two scales, perception and importance, unlike LibQUAL+, which uses three scales in order to assess their 'zone of tolerance'.

This methodology has been predominantly used by Australian academic libraries after the Council of Australian University Librarians (CAUL; www.caul.edu.au/) negotiated a consortium pricing model in 2007 (Gallagher, 2015). CAUL members have access to a portal providing survey results to enable benchmarking. For each of the five categories the top five libraries are provided, along with sector averages and customised comparator groups. Case Study 3.2 looks at how the Insync survey is used at the University of Sydney.

Ithaka S+R

The Ithaka S+R surveys have been used predominantly by academic libraries in the USA, but also in Canada and the UK. They provide three separate surveys for different customer groups: undergraduate, graduate and faculty. The surveys offer a combination of core questions for benchmarking purposes, and optional question areas (or modules) to enable local customisation. All three have one common set of questions on 'the role of the library'. The undergraduate and graduate surveys focus on the academic goals of the respondent and their coursework, with questions tailored appropriately for each audience. The faculty survey naturally differs in its focus, exploring research practices and discovery and use of scholarly collections in academia.

The Ithaka S+R survey uses a combination of frequency questions with response options ranging from 'never' to 'often'; and statement questions with a Likert 1–10 scale, which are commonly used in survey methodology (Habib et al., 2014). The results of the statement questions are grouped into broader categories at the analysis stage, for example 'extremely important' or 'not at all important'. With the standardised methodology comparisons between peer institutions and sector or national averages are available with this survey. The faculty survey in particular has been used since 2000, although the questions asked have adjusted to the changing information provision landscape over time. The methodology has consistently measured the needs, perceptions and practices of faculty members in their teaching and research. In recent years questions have evolved to also explore practices and perceptions around research data management, open access and learning analytics (Wolff-Eisenberg, 2018). Case Study 3.3 describes how local Ithaka S+R surveys have been used at the UNLV libraries.

The MISO Survey

The Measuring Information Services Outcomes (MISO) Survey (www.misosurvey.org/) is predominantly used in North America and provides insight into library and information technology services in the same instrument. Originally developed by David Consiglio and team at the Bryn Mawr College (Allen et al., 2013), the survey was later adopted by the Council for Library and Information Resources and has been used there since 2005. As the boundaries between library and information technology provision in higher education have become blurred, or fully converged, the MISO Survey is designed to meet this combined assessment need. Like the surveys previously described it asks respondents about their perceptions and expectations of the item being evaluated. Participants can add custom and bespoke questions to the core instrument, which is circulated via a web-based survey to faculty, university staff and a sample of students. Unusually the survey deployment is co-ordinated between participating institutions to strengthen the comparability of the results between them (Allen et al., 2013).

Case Study 3.1 LibQUAL+ as a catalyst for change at the University of Limerick
Ciara McCaffrey and Michelle Breen

Introduction
In 2002, as LibQUAL+ was in its infancy, Tom B. Wall prophesised that libraries deciding to participate in LibQUAL+ might use the experience as 'a critical first step in a longitudinal analysis of library collections and systems. With the commitment to listening to users and rethinking the service program, the LibQUAL+ process is inherently transformative' (Wall, 2002). The University of Limerick (UL), located in the west of Ireland, took this critical step by running LibQUAL+ for the first time in 2007, and in doing so began a programme of change, continuous improvement and systematic assessment that spanned a decade and transformed library services. This case study will outline the contribution that LibQUAL+ played to the transformation and the long-lasting impact the survey has had on library services at the UL.

One of seven universities in the Republic of Ireland, the UL is a relatively young institution with a history of innovation, entrepreneurship and excellence in education, research and scholarship. The UL provides undergraduate and postgraduate degrees across a broad range of disciplines including science, technology, engineering and maths (STEM), business, education, health sciences, social sciences, arts and humanities. The student population of UL grew steadily since its foundation in 1972, reaching 15,000 by 2016, of which 2,300 were postgraduates. The mission of the Glucksman Library is to support the teaching, learning and research activities of the UL by providing quality information resources, education, support and facilities to students, faculty, staff and researchers. The Library is one of the most popular and heavily used resources on campus, with over 1 million in-person visits annually and 1.5 million digital downloads from the collection, which comprises 600,000 print and e-books and 62,000 e-journals.

The Library was built in 1997 with 1,100 study seats to accommodate a student population of 7,000. By 2007, when the library ran LibQUAL+ for the first time, the student population had grown substantially, placing increasing pressure on limited space and resources. A new library director and a changing management group saw the LibQUAL+ survey as a new opportunity for students and faculty of the university to give large-scale feedback on all aspects of library service. Library leadership had a change agenda that was outward-facing and informed by developments internationally, with a strong appreciation of where the library needed to go. LibQUAL+ was part of this change agenda, while also enabling it. The tool was relatively easy to deploy, did not require significant expertise or resourcing to implement, generated a large body of quantitative and qualitative user survey data, was rigorously tested, and provided a powerful capacity for benchmarking locally, nationally and internationally.

The 2007 survey results provided irrefutable evidence of the need for change by highlighting that respondents had substantial difficulties with the building and the collections; a major noise problem and the unavailability of core texts were at the top of a long list of issues for library users. The results and survey comments were shared with library staff who were encouraged to view them as a call to action and an exciting opportunity to meet our users' needs better. A LibQUAL+ action plan was put in place, consisting of small- and medium-scale improvements, which were implemented as part of library planning. Two years later, the UL ran LibQUAL+ again and somewhat nervously awaited the results. In 2009 user satisfaction had increased – the relatively modest action plan appeared to have had impact with library users. Changes in the two-year period had made a difference. Encouraged by the experience, the library entered into a cycle of measure–improve–measure, using LibQUAL+ as the measurement tool and now runs the survey every two years.

The first venture into LibQUAL+ began a programme of change, continuous improvement and systematic assessment, which spanned a decade and transformed library services at the UL.

Acting on LibQUAL+

LibQUAL+ is now a cornerstone of the Library's continuous improvement programme and a key enabler of evidence-based decision making. Over the years, the integration of the results with the library's strategic and planning cycle has matured and deepened. The survey is deployed every two years by the librarian (administration), overseen by the deputy librarian. After each survey, the results are analysed by cross-referencing the areas that are most highly prioritised by the different user groups (desired means) with the areas where respondents feel we are performing below minimum requirements (adequacy means). The qualitative comments are coded into categories such as space, collections, borrowing, security, staff, and so on. The results, including comments, are shared with all library staff. Analysis of the results has become more advanced as staff competence has increased, and includes internal longitudinal benchmarking, external benchmarking with national and international data, and intensive focus on particular user groups or issues that arise at any given time.

The Library's Quality Review Group, a team of staff representing all departments and grades across the library and chaired by the deputy librarian, monitors quality activities and progress. It considers the LibQUAL+ results and makes recommendations for quality improvements. These are then considered by the Library Management Group, led by the director of Library & Information Services. From these activities, a quality action plan is developed and integrated with the library's planning and quality cycles. Actions in the plan are assigned ownership to one of the heads of department and funding is allocated if required. The action plan is monitored by the Quality Review Group quarterly and reviewed twice yearly by the Library Management Group. When an action is complete it is removed from the plan and added to the 'You said, we did' record on the library website. In addition to the action plan, the results influence overall strategy by identifying the need for change more broadly in one of the three dimensions or the need for a different approach with particular user groups.

The programme of change from 2007 to 2017

A great many changes occurred at the UL Library over the period 2007–17; some were direct outcomes of LibQUAL+ while others arose from the change agenda set by wider strategy. Significant investment was directed towards developing collections, spaces and services. A planned library extension was postponed a number of times, therefore efforts were focused on improving existing space as much as possible. A building refurbishment, involving glazing noisy atriums and installing doors throughout reading rooms, dealt to some extent with environmental issues. Library space was reorganised to better deliver study areas that enabled diverse activities, such as silent, quiet, group and collaborative work, and a desig-nated postgraduate reading room was created. Technological advancements included a book sorter, access gates, improved self-service machines, wired connections at all study desks and Wi-fi throughout the building. The library's noise problem, so clearly articulated by students in multiple LibQUAL+ surveys, was dealt with through a series of interventions which are outlined in detail in McCaffrey and Breen (2016).

Information resources were developed by creating subject-level collection develop-ment policies and by targeted investment in recommended reading, textbooks and e-books. The Irish Research eLibrary (IReL; www.irelibrary.ie/) initiative – a national purchasing arrangement – led to a major expansion of electronic resources for Irish research libraries. IReL enabled UL's electronic journal collection to almost double from 32,000 in 2007 to 62,000 in 2016.

In the same period the library's technical services processes were automated, research support services were developed, digitisation and digital services were established and a major expansion of the library's special collections and archives occurred. An economic recession had a very significant impact on the library during the period, leading to reductions in staffing levels and budgets. Staffed services were reorganised to provide information support, while staffed circulation activities were replaced by self-service facilities. Appendix 1 details the main improvements that occurred from the quality action plans generated following each LibQUAL+ survey.

Users' perceptions of library services

The UL LibQUAL+ results from 2007 to 2017 reflect how users perceived this programme of change and tell a compelling story of a commitment to improvement that is user-centred, continuous and systematic. In the five iterations of the survey, the UL LibQUAL+ user scores have consistently risen, increasing in all areas measured – staffing, collections and spaces. The steady increase in positive ratings of library services by students demonstrates that the improvement programme has been successful and that library users are much more satisfied with services in 2017 than they were a decade previously.

The impact of LibQUAL+

The impact of LibQUAL+ on the UL is manifold and has brought various benefits to the library over the last decade. The survey puts the user at the heart of continuous improvement and this has created a strong ethos of customer service among library staff. The recognition and appreciation of the great many improvements the library has made over the years is apparent in the qualitative comments that have been received through the survey. LibQUAL+ has enabled the library to deliver a consistent message and to develop an excellent ongoing relationship with the student body, and has contributed to a reputation for responsiveness that stands out in the university. The continually improving survey results provide evidence to university management that the division knows what it is doing and is in control of its brief.

The survey has been an extremely useful part of the library's quality management system, a framework established for all support divisions in the university. Customer focus is a primary element of the UL's quality management system, and the LibQUAL+ survey is one of the library's key methods to gather and respond to feedback from users. The principle measure–improve–measure, facilitated by LibQUAL+, is a central element of the library's quality processes.

There is little doubt that regular running of the survey and its integration with the planning cycle has contributed to a culture of assessment in the library. Lakos and Phipps (2004) defined this as 'an organizational environment in which decisions are based on facts, research and analysis and where services are planned and delivered in ways that maximise positive outcomes and impacts for customers'. This culture is present at all levels and in all departments across UL Library. A strong record of action research as part of the library's assessment activities and quality management system has developed. In addition to customer feedback, an array of usage and performance data is gathered systematically, analysed and acted on to enable evidence-based continuous improvement. While there are no staff fully dedicated to assessment, as confidence has grown with survey administration and analysis, other research methods have been added to the library's assessment activities, including in-house surveys, focus groups and user experience methods.

LibQUAL+ and managing change

LibQUAL+ has had most impact as a change management tool. The sizeable user feedback that comes from the survey has been powerful when making the case for change, whether with university management, staff or library users. As a change management tool LibQUAL+ in UL:

- empowered us to make decisive change
- provided detail on where to change and on where improvements were most needed
- provided support when change was unpopular
- deflected opposition to change
- enabled us to challenge outdated preconceptions relating to users, collections and spaces held by some faculty and staff
- provided an opportunity to raise issues at the highest levels of the university
- crucially, normalised change for library staff.

Going forward

From the perspective of users, library services at the UL significantly improved from where they were in 2007 and further transformation is planned. A major building project is under way that will increase the library by two-thirds and is scheduled for completion in 2018. The 2016 LibQUAL+ survey provides a baseline with which to measure the impact of the new building. The 2018 survey will provide a post-occupancy opportunity to evaluate the impact on library users and identify opportunities for further improvement. The user feedback on the library environment gathered over many years has informed the planning of this space. The transformed library will provide technology-rich, creative and inspirational spaces to meet current and future needs. The aim is not just to add extra space but to create an outstanding facility that will provide for the needs of the university long into the future and distinguish UL as an innovative and pioneering institution.

As Wall (2002) predicted, implementing the LibQUAL+ process has been inherently transformative at the UL. The programme of change, continuous improvement and systematic assessment, which originated with LibQUAL+ and spanned a decade, is set to continue the transformation of library services at the UL well into the future.

Appendix: Improvements that followed LibQUAL+ action plans

We made the following improvements between 2007 and 2009:

- targeted investment on core texts and recommended reading
- centralised all services points to single service area
- introduced new self-service facilities
- created a silent area on floor 2, identified phone-friendly areas, increased staff patrols
- ran a noise campaign, issued guidelines to staff and library users
- introduced 'recommend a book' and 'request a missing item' services
- introduced a 'compliments, comments, complaints' process

- introduced a book returns box at the entrance
- improved the online public access catalogue equipment
- improved signage on all shelves
- introduced liquid-crystal display (LCD) screens to provide digital signage to customers.

We made the following improvements between 2009 and 2012:

- targeted book funds towards reading list material and e-book versions
- refurbished the building to glaze atria and install doors into reading areas
- increased and relocated self-service facilities to a more visible library entrance
- renovated and relocated all desk services to a one-stop shop at a more visible library entrance
- connected every study desk and group study room with power and data points
- provided full Wi-fi throughout the library
- introduced the 'ask us' online query service
- introduced library Facebook and Twitter communications with customers
- introduced the Summon discovery tool
- introduced an e-payments facility for borrowers to pay fines online
- introduced texting service to alert borrowers when loans are due back
- converted library collections to radio-frequency identification (RFID)
- introduced a student peer adviser service to support new students.

We made the following improvements between 2012 and 2014:

- created a postgraduate reading room
- zoned all areas of library (silent, quiet, group, phone)
- relocated and increased silent zones and increased space for group work
- increased borrower entitlements
- extended opening hours of high-use short loan collections
- developed an extensive training programme for information desk staff
- employed a student noise monitor
- introduced staff name badges
- updated library floor plans
- streamlined and improved 'access from home' login procedures
- created new 'how to' documentation and redesigned existing forms and guides
- increased Wi-fi routers and improved wired connections at desks
- introduced a librarian consultation desk for high-level queries.

We made the following improvements between 2014 and 2016:

- developed 26 collection development policies in collaboration with all academic departments
- completed a journal review to assess usage, cost per download, etc.
- introduced a new post of librarian, research & bibliometrics
- developed a research skills programme called Realising Your Research Value
- developed the UL Institutional Repository
- extended library opening hours approaching exam time
- installed a book sorter for automated book returns
- installed access gates to improve security and access to building
- introduced a new post of librarian, student engagement & success to assist new students
- broadened and developed the student peer adviser scheme
- introduced an online booking system for group study rooms
- introduced a desk clearing project to release space by removing belongings from unattended seats.

Case Study 3.2 The Insync survey at the University of Sydney
Belinda Norman

Introduction

The University of Sydney is one of Australia's leading research institutions, with approximately 60,000 undergraduate student enrolments, 3,000 higher degree students and 3,350 academic staff. The University is ranked in the top 100 universities globally (University of Sydney, 2018). Research, teaching and learning is pursued across the full range of scholarly endeavour and takes place across nine campuses, clustered primarily in central Sydney, but also extending into a number of rural and regional campuses. The uUniversity is currently engaged in a process of transformation as described in the 2016–20 Strategic Plan, which seeks outlines the University's vision to 'create and sustain a university in which, for the benefit of Australia and the wider world, the brightest researchers and the most promising students, whatever their social or cultural background, can thrive and realise their potential' (University of Sydney, 2016).

The University of Sydney Library is embedded in and actively enriches the student and research lifecycles, working in collaboration with partners across the university to deliver on the University's research and education outcomes. It delivers services across 12 library sites on 6 campuses. We provide scholarly information resources that are discoverable, accessible and fit for purpose to enable and underpin teaching and research. We design and manage a range of informal, flexible and inclusive learning spaces to inspire learning, spark creativity and foster collaboration. We work in partnership to deliver professional advice and tailored programmes to develop digital and information literacies and increase research visibility, accessibility and impact. We foster the creation and dissemination of knowledge through our scholarship infrastructure and services. The Library's culture, activities and services are grounded in the University's values and centred on the needs of our client communities.

Survey background

Kent and Samarchi (2009) point to a 'long history of measurement and usage of statistics by library managers' in Australia. This was the foundation for a smattering of service quality initiatives, which emerged across the mid to late 1990s in Australian academic libraries (Kent and Samarchi, 2009). These developments eventually culminated in the development and implementation of a standard survey instrument for libraries in 2001 by the Council of Australian University Librarians (CAUL).

A common approach would assist university libraries to have a common set of performance indicators and 'facilitate the potential for benchmarking and cross-organisational learning' (Kent and Samarchi, 2009). Individual institutions can add additional customised questions to assess performance on a local level, in addition to the standard suite that underpins the benchmarking data.

CAUL member organisations have access to the Library Client Survey Benchmark Portal since 2013, where benchmark data for participating libraries is made available. The University of Sydney Library could run a benchmark against other Group of Eight universities to see our relative performance against similar institutions, with the caveat that our survey results may not have been gathered in a comparable timeframe. Another approach would be to take a particular category as a frame and explore the highest performers in that category across the sector, or within our region.

Our history with the survey

The University of Sydney Library has conducted the Insync Library Client Survey (formerly Rodksi Survey) seven times since 2002, as part of the CAUL and later CAUL or the Council of New Zealand University Librarians consortium commitment to understanding and improving the needs and experiences of their client communities.

The tool primarily captures the response of students, most of whom are undergraduates. In the last ten years undergraduate responses have comprised on average 58% of the total. Other cohorts respond on average as follows: postgraduate coursework students 17%, postgraduate research students 11.94%, and academic research staff 7.18%.

How we conducted the survey

The University of Sydney Library most recently conducted the Insync Library Client Survey in September 2016, the first since 2013 and covering a period of significant organisational change. This change delivered major innovations in delivery of services to client communities, in particular a holistic and transformative redesign of library spaces and service models, including the introduction of 24/7 opening across a number of sites.

Given that context, the library executive chose to include customised questions, beyond the primary generic set that provides the basis for inter-institutional benchmarking, focused on client experience in our transformed spaces, associated service models and 24/7 opening.

The survey was accompanied by an intensive burst of marketing including social media, entries in the student newsletter, website, posters and digital signage in library sites and other student-focused locations across campus. In high-traffic library sites we set up lunch time survey stations with tables and iPads for students to complete the survey and provided fruit and lollies as incentives. Those who completed the survey were eligible to enter the draw to win a first prize of AUS$1000 (approximately equivalent to US$750 or £550). At the close of the two-week survey period we had received 2976 responses, a figure more or less consistent with responses received to the last four surveys.

How we use results

The Insync results prompted a range of sessions where senior managers shared the findings with the wider library staff and pinpointed projects to address gaps identified in the survey report. The Insync survey data has been deployed to support business cases, and advocate for student needs in a range of strategic and tactical scenarios over the period in which we have undertaken the survey. Survey summary reports were made available on the library website and top ten areas of importance and performance were highlighted. The full survey data report was broken down into summary sections, to provide snapshots by faculty and library site and made available to library staff, including the project groups, along with verbatim comments, categorised by themes. The project groups took categories as their frame and undertook more detailed analysis of the verbatim comments. They also reached out to best performing libraries in their categories to hear more about their successful approaches. This process often laid bare the limitations of the benchmarking when groups discovered that those high performing libraries were at institutions whose size, scale and complexity was not comparable with Sydney.

Insync data in 2013 showed a gap between importance and performance for the statement 'opening hours meet my needs'. Combined with benchmarking data for that statement across the industry, that data was used to illustrate how we were falling below industry standards. Most influential however was a photograph taken of students lining up outside the library awaiting entry, which demonstrated for us that it takes more than numbers to tell a powerful story. A pilot initiative opening space in one section of the biggest site, Fisher Library, 24/7 was launched. This 24/7 project acted as an incubator and proof of concept for the library to build a successful case for larger-scale 24/7 opening across a number of sites, including Fisher in its entirety.

At a more tactical level, Insync data has been used to make cases for improved services where we work in partnership with other units to deliver services into library spaces. For example data which showed poor Wi-fi performance was used to help influence our IT department to improve Wi-fi infrastructure in library spaces, turning this from a low performing to a high performing area in subsequent surveys. Similarly Insync data, in this case the compelling verbatim comments, has helped communicate the need for improved cleanliness in library spaces to our facilities management unit.

To a certain extent the Insync survey data is also used by library staff to advocate for student needs in a complex environment with multiple stakeholders and varying priorities. Insync data has been used recently in conversations with academic staff about research collections, to ensure student needs stay on the table. Data from the 2016 survey shows a distinct shift in what students value from collections to spaces, which the library has used to underpin a case for introducing more holistic management of informal study spaces across the university.

The 2016 results showed there was an overall improvement in client satisfaction across all of the categories that structure the survey. Of the gap areas identified, none were within the critical range. In contrast to the organisational context in 2013, in 2016 we were a year into a new organisational structure and in the process of shaping a strategic plan, closely aligned with the university's strategic plan, and with a strong client focus, which will take us through to the end of the decade. To inform the development of the plan, we undertook additional qualitative client engagements to investigate what is important to our client groups in more depth. Given the holistic and strategic, client-centred roadmap that our new strategic plan delivered us, we felt confident that additional responsive projects to address gap areas identified by the Insync data were not a strategic priority in 2016. The major gaps identified – around physical library spaces and facilities – merely served to confirm challenges we were already well aware of and already working systematically to address.

Data gathered from the 2016 survey was used to update a set of design thinking personas the library has developed as a tool when scoping and targeting new initiatives. Staff sessions were held to share overall responses and to encourage teams to interrogate and access the data at point of need.

The value of assessment

The main value for us delivered by historical and continued use of the survey is the ability to benchmark our performance against that of other institutions over time. It also serves an important function as the only client survey tool we use routinely and systematically, thus ensuring that we are regularly made aware of our clients' views on our everyday services. The inter-institutional benchmarking has its limitations. For example, it is anecdotally understood that the performance of smaller institutions generally fares better than that of larger ones, so the limitations of comparing large, multi-campus institutions that serve 60,000 students with smaller organisations becomes apparent. However the tool has been valuable as a means to identify high performing libraries in different areas, and as a lever for inter-organisational connection and shared learning.

Crucial as well is the survey's ability to map the trajectory of what's important to respondents over time, within the constraints of the survey's frame. For example, between 2013 and 2016 they gradually ranked spaces as more important to them than resources.

Future opportunities

To date, we have not undertaken a more detailed analysis of data to map and visualise our performance, and what is important to our clients over time. Some trends are visible to the naked eye – our staff services are consistently ranked as our highest performing category for example – but other valuable insights are also no doubt hidden in the data.

The challenge remains to make the best use of the data, maximising the value of the investment, within a broader framework of engagement to enable us to build towards our strategic goal to engage staff and students as co-designers and co-creators of University Library services, spaces, collections and programmes. To a certain extent, once received the data is discussed and examined, but then almost neglected until the next survey period rolls around. We aspire to embed the data more thoroughly in the way we do business so we consult survey data, appropriate to the task in hand (e.g. taking the appropriate slice either by faculty, library location or client type), as a natural and routine first step in a process of ensuring that what we're embarking on is client focused, and that we address clients' needs when undertaking any particular task. In that way, the library client survey can serve as a kind of stepping stone to a purposeful and firm commitment by library staff to close client engagement. Once the data is consulted, teams can then conduct further qualitative investigations using a range of methodologies such as user experience and design thinking research tools, world cafés and other engagement approaches, as explored in other chapters within this book.

The questions posed by the Insync client survey are important but narrow. There are other, more interesting questions that we need to be asking our clients. For example, Insync asks 'what do you need from the Library?'; perhaps a more interesting question, and the one we need to ask in addition, is 'what do you need to thrive?' The answers to that question are the gateway to delivering more value to the mission of the university and our clients, and in asking that question raising the potential of libraries in our minds and those of our clients.

Case Study 3.3 Ithaka S+R local surveys at the UNLV Libraries
Starr Hoffman

In fall 2015, the University of Nevada, Las Vegas (UNLV) Libraries conducted three local surveys designed and administered by Ithaka S+R (www.sr.ithaka.org/). Each survey targeted a different population: faculty (asking about their research practices), undergraduates (asking about their academic experience and library satisfaction) and graduate students (asking about their research practices and levels of satisfaction with the library). For each survey, Ithaka S+R offers a core questionnaire, and additional optional question sets on different themes (for instance, you can add a section on scholarly communication to the faculty survey).

The context of the UNLV libraries

The UNLV is an urban research-focused university located in Las Vegas, Nevada, USA. In part due to its location in a highly diverse major city, UNLV's student body is incredibly diverse culturally and ethnically. It is among the youngest large institutions of higher education in the USA, having been established in 1957, and has grown to a student body of over 30,000 with nearly 4000 FTE faculty. UNLV's mission focuses on its role as a 'top tier' public university with a particular focus on research and community impact.

The UNLV libraries support this top tier mission through their mission to define 'the new academic research library' and strategic focus on research support, student achievement and community engagement (UNLV University Libraries, n.d.). The libraries employ 130 full-time equivalent faculty and staff (including 56 tenure-track and tenured librarians) and have five physical branch locations: Lied Library (the main building), the Architecture Studies Library, the Health Sciences Library, the Music Library and the Teacher Development and Resources Library.

Why Ithaka S+R?

For several cycles in the 2000s, the UNLV libraries had used the LibQUAL+ instrument. However, after there were low response rates to a lengthy survey, in 2012 the libraries developed a shorter, more focused local user survey. When considering in 2015 how to survey library users about their needs related to their research and strategic institutional initiatives, the libraries considered using LibQUAL+ and a locally developed user survey alongside the Ithaka S+R surveys.

Ultimately, the UNLV libraries chose the Ithaka surveys for several reasons. First, as mentioned above, UNLV's current focus is on a 'top tier' strategic plan to increase institutional research and community impact. In order to determine how best to support UNLV's research needs, the libraries needed more information about research practices and faculty needs. Specifically, the libraries were interested in what kinds of activities faculty engaged in and types of resources they used in their research, and any gaps they found in support services or research resources. The Ithaka faculty survey questions fitted these needs well, providing much relevant information with which library staff could make decisions. This information allowed us to identify emerging needs and potential new directions, in contrast to the more traditional service focus of the LibQUAL+ survey and local instrument.

Second, the libraries has generally surveyed library users every second or third fall semester. As the Ithaka surveys encompassed several areas which the regular survey generally covers (such as faculty satisfaction with collections and services, and student satisfaction with services and spaces), they seemed a fair substitute for the existing survey. This allowed us to address research support needs in one set of surveys and the libraries' regular user assessment, rather than increase survey fatigue by administering the usual user survey and the Ithaka survey later in the same year.

Survey administration

One of the advantages of using the Ithaka S+R surveys was their facilitation of the survey administration process. Ithaka S+R staff sent the invitation e-mails, advised on how to increase response rates, sent staggered reminder messages, and branded the survey with our institution name and logo. After the survey was closed, Ithaka S+R provided full reports with graphical and tabular results and the raw data set. These full reports were quite basic, so we used the raw data to run more in-depth analyses in Tableau, but having initial results quickly was helpful. We paid for Ithaka to write three executive summaries (one for each survey), focused on topics and findings that we selected. Finally, Ithaka sent us a final report on the faculty survey, comparing our data with that of our Carnegie classification peers from the national data set. Carnegie classification is the framework for describing institutional diversity in US higher education (Carnegie Classification of Institutions of Higher Education, n.d.)

Barriers and lessons learned

One of the few frustrating aspects of the Ithaka S+R surveys was that inconsistent Likert answer scales made interpreting and communicating some results difficult. For instance, in the faculty survey, question 14 on publication services provided a Likert scale with ten answer options, while question 22 on tenure offered only a seven-item Likert answer scale. Because of this, comparing means over a sequence of questions was difficult to interpret and analyse in a succinct and understandable way. Reporting the results narratively was also difficult because many of the answer scales provided text (such as 'extremely valuable' or 'not at all valuable') for only the beginning and end points of the scale. Thus, instead of being able to report digestible results in narrative reports, we had to resort to either reporting means (which are imprecise for Likert data and often difficult to understand for a broad audience) or providing unwieldy lists of percentages and numbers. To make this information easier to digest, we imported the raw data into Tableau to create a series of visualisations, primarily stacked bar charts.

One lesson we learned was to choose fewer of the optional modules. An overview of the survey sections used by UNLV Libraries in fall 2015 can be seen in the appendix to this case study. The core questionnaire for the faculty survey in particular is already long; the three optional modules that we added (18 questions) resulted in quite a few faculty comments about survey length (although our response rate was still 5% higher than our previous highest faculty survey response rate). We chose the optional modules because they were on topics relevant to our needs (e.g. scholarly communication), and we wanted to pull as much information as possible out of a single survey. In retrospect, however, not all of the modules delivered enough valuable information to justify further lengthening the survey. Additionally, a confusing aspect of the modules is that some explore topics that are initially mentioned in the core survey. Some respondents were confused to answer a question about scholarly communication, then many unrelated questions, and then find a set of scholarly communication questions related to the first one much later. If Ithaka S+R could provide an option to thematically group related questions from optional modules this would greatly enhance their usability.

Using survey results

Despite the issues mentioned above, the results of the surveys were fairly useful, particularly the faculty survey. Over the past two years they informed a variety of initiatives across the libraries and have been instrumental in our planning of research support students for faculty and students, illustrating service gaps as well as our existing strengths. As UNLV increases its research capacity it has been important for the libraries to understand faculty and student research practices. For instance, the Ithaka surveys ask questions about types of materials used for original research and literature reviews, which have helped us make decisions about collection development and software support for various statistical applications. Survey results also pointed out differences in research needs by disciplinary areas and showed the need for more education about open access. The ambiguity of the questions on data support led us to conduct additional research into what respondents define 'data' to be (e.g. research data or secondary data) via focus groups and other means.

Once the results were analysed by academic area, our liaison (subject expert) librarians found them useful for constructing accreditation statements in their areas, such as, '70% of graduate students in the College of Allied Health Sciences find the libraries' collections to be extremely useful, and another 21% find them very useful.' These college-specific results are particularly valuable because although we do a lot of assessment at the UNLV Libraries, little of what we gather is separated by the users' academic area, and results are thus less useful to individual colleges and schools seeking re-accreditation.

The three Ithaka surveys taken as a whole have guided the UNLV Libraries' strategic goals, which are nested within the university's strategic plan. This plan is called 'top tier' for its emphasis on increasing research productivity and quality to increase UNLV's reputation and potentially gain status as a 'Tier 1' or 'Research 1' institution in the Carnegie classification. The emphasis on 'top tier' quality extends beyond research to the areas of teaching, supporting underserved populations, and more, though increasing research is a top area of focus. The libraries' strategic objectives are nested within the five goals from the university's top tier plan, covering:

- research, scholarship and creative activity
- student achievement
- a new medical school (and associated health sciences library)
- community partnerships
- infrastructure (UNLV, n.d.).

The Ithaka survey results have particularly helped the libraries determine how to support the first goal area better, increased research activity for faculty and students alike. For instance, survey results related to faculty and student needs in data visualisation, virtual reality and other emerging technologies resulted in the creation of a new library department, Knowledge Production, which seeks to immerse these technologies within the curriculum. The senior leadership team and the head of this new department have used Ithaka data extensively in exploring the need for this area, and continue to use it while planning new services and spaces.

Collaboration and data sharing
Each of the Ithaka surveys encompasses topics beyond the scope of the libraries; this is particularly true of the undergraduate and graduate student surveys. For instance, both student surveys have a section on higher education objectives, where there are questions on how important various aspects of post-secondary education, such as study abroad or participation in social events, are to the respondent. This broad scope provided negative and positive outcomes: a lengthy survey makes us reluctant to use this tool frequently; more positively, by sharing results that are out of scope for the libraries with partners in areas such as the Graduate College and Undergraduate Education we have opened conversations across campus. These conversations have strengthened our existing collaborations with these offices, and renewed conversations about partnering on campus-wide surveys to reduce survey fatigue and increase response rates.

National comparisons
The faculty survey is particularly valuable for benchmarking, as Ithaka S+R has administered the US faculty survey every three years since 2000. This gave us the opportunity to compare UNLV's results with those of faculty from similar doctoral universities across the USA. The comparable data was gathered in the same year (Wolff, Rod and Schonfeld, 2016a). For our comparison purposes, Ithaka S+R provided us a data set pre-filtered only to include universities within UNLV's Carnegie classification: doctoral universities and higher research activity. This subset of data included 1622 respondents from institutions in that Carnegie classification. The report provided to us had analysed these respondents in the aggregate, rather than separating by institution or other methods.

Because this analysis was similar to the UNLV-specific analysis that Ithaka S+R previously provided, we were able to make comparisons by viewing the reports side by side to get a general sense of key similarities or differences from our peer institutions. Many of our results fell squarely within our peer group, which is as we expect and largely what we desire. Some of the areas where we fell slightly outside the norm were interesting, for instance, nearly twice as many UNLV faculty shared research online under Creative Commons or open source licensing (13.36%) compared with the national group (7.39%).

Appendix: Ithaka S+R local survey sections

There were three survey sections in the Ithaka S+R survey on UNLV Libraries in fall 2015.
The undergraduate survey covered:

- higher education objectives
- coursework and academics
- role of the library
- library space planning (optional)
- extra- and co-curricular experiences (optional)
- undergraduate research activities (optional)
- demographic details.

The graduate student survey covered:

- higher education objectives
- coursework and academics
- role of the library
- library space planning (optional)
- research practices (optional)
- teaching (optional)
- demographic details.

The faculty survey covered:

- discovery and access, scholarly communications, student research skills, research practices and the role of the library
- data preservation and management (optional)
- scholarly communications (optional)
- library market research (optional)
- demographic details.

Conclusions

In this chapter we have seen how standardised surveys can be used by libraries to assess their current provision with limited time needed to develop the methodology. Their unique strength is the ability to compare performance between peer libraries and national or cohort averages to put local results in context. Both LibQUAL+ and Insync have developed their methodologies from the commercial product SERVQUAL. The Ithaka survey has grown from national research into information provision. The finding from the surveys can be used to improve the library for its various customer groups providing the insight gained is acted on to improve service provision.

References

Allen, L., Baker, N., Wilson, J., Creamer, K. and Consiglio, D. (2013) Analyzing the MISO Data: Broader Perspectives on Library and Computing Trends, *Evidence Based Library and Information Practice*, **8** (82), 129–38, doi: http://dx.doi.org/10.18438/B82G7V.

Carnegie Classification of Institutions of Higher Education (n.d.) *About Carnegie Classification*, http://carnegieclassifications.iu.edu/.

Cook, C. and Heath, F. (2001) Users' Perceptions of Library Service Quality: a LibQUAL+ qualitative study, *Library Trends*, **49** (4), 548–84.

Cook, C., Heath, F. and Thompson, B. (2002) LibQUAL+: one instrument in the new measures toolbox, *Journal of Library Administration*, **35** (4), 41–6, doi: 10.1300/J111v35n04_09.

Creaser, C. (2006) One Size Does Not Fit All: user surveys in academic libraries, *Performance Measurement and Metrics*, **7** (3), 153–62, doi: 10.1108/14678040610713110.

Gallagher, A. (2015) *Comparison of Library Surveys: Insync, LibQual+, Ithaka*, Council of Australian University Libraries, www.caul.edu.au/caul-programs/best-practice/performance-indicators.

Group of Eight (2018) *Group of Eight: about*, https://go8.edu.au/page/about.

Habib, M. M., Pathik, B. B., Maryam, H. and Habib, M. (2014) *Research Methodology – Contemporary Practices: guidelines for academic researchers*, Cambridge Scholars Publishing, http://ebookcentral.proquest.com/lib/open/detail.action?docID=1819209.

Kent, P. G. and Samarchi, M. (2009) Show Me the Data: increasing client satisfaction. In *ALIA Information Online 2009, 14th Exhibition & Conference*, http://vuir.vu.edu.au/1969/.

Lakos, A. and Phipps, S. (2004) Creating a Culture of Assessment: a catalyst for organizational change, *Portal: Libraries and the Academy*, **4** (3), 345–61, http://escholarship.org/uc/item/0843106w.

McCaffrey, C. and Breen, M. (2016) Quiet in the Library: an evidence-based approach to improving the student experience, *Portal: Libraries and the Academy*, **16** (4), 775–91, doi: 10.1353/pla.2016.0052.

Revill, D. and Ford, G. (1996) *User Satisfaction: standard survey forms for academic libraries*. Society of College, National and University Libraries.

Trahn, I., Croud, J., Kealy, K. and Hayward, J. (2001) Analysing the Quality Gap: reflections on results from an Australasian Universitas 21 libraries standard survey of service quality, *Australian Academic and Research Libraries*, **32** (2), 93–109, doi: 10.1080/00048623.2001.10755149.

University of Sydney (2016) *2016–20 Strategic Plan*, https://sydney.edu.au/about-us/vision-and-values/strategy.html.

University of Sydney (2018) *Our World University Rankings: The University of Sydney*, https://sydney.edu.au/about-us/our-world-rankings.html.

UNLV (n.d.) Top Tier Plan, https://www.unlv.edu/toptier.

UNLV University Libraries (n.d.) Strategic Framework July 2017 – June 2019, https://www.library.unlv.edu/sites/default/files/documents/pages/admin_stratplan20172019_finalized20170829.pdf

Van House, N. A., Weil, B. T. and McClure, C. R. (1990) *Measuring Academic Library Performance: a practical approach*, American Library Association.

Wall, T. B. (2002) LibQUAL+ as Transformative Experience, *Performance Measurement and Metrics*, **3** (2), 43–8, doi: 10.1108/14678040210440928.

West, C. (2004) *User Surveys in UK and Irish HE Libraries*. Society of College, National and University Libraries.

Wolff, C., Rod, A. B. and Schonfeld, R. C. (2016a) *Ithaka S + R US Faculty Survey 2015*, *Ithaka S+R*, doi: 10.18655/sr.282736.

Wolff, C., Rod, A. B. and Schonfeld, R. C. (2016b) *Ithaka S+R, Jisc, RLUK UK Survey of Academics 2015*, doi: 10.18665/sr.277685.

Wolff-Eisenberg, C. (2018) *New Questionnaire for the US Faculty Survey 2018 Now Available*, www.sr.ithaka.org/blog/new-questionnaire-for-the-us-faculty-survey-2018-now-available/.

Chapter 4

In-house library surveys

Chapter overview

In this chapter we will discuss the use of locally designed and administered surveys and how they can be used to improve libraries. One of the key concepts discussed in the previous chapter on standardised surveys is echoed here – the use of survey methodologies to evaluate customers' expectations and perceptions – but the two approaches have different advantages and disadvantages. Standardised surveys are designed by a team, and often some level of analysis is conducted by the tool, saving the library time and money. Library staff design and analyse in-house surveys. And whereas a standardised survey provides a generic set of questions to enable comparisons to be made between institutions, an in-house survey can provide greater insight by focusing on local issues. Before you embark on a local or a standardised survey, we recommend you identify your strategic needs and determine which methodology suits your library best.

This chapter presents four case studies on how local surveys have been developed and implemented to improve customers' experience at academic libraries:

- Case Study 4.1 Beyond answering questions: designing actionable surveys to guide assessment, make decisions and support ongoing analysis (Jackie Belanger, Maggie Faber and Steve Hiller)
- Case Study 4.2 Taking users' opinions into account when managing an academic library: a decade in retrospect (Tatiana Sanches)
- Case Study 4.3 Giving students voice: a biennial user satisfaction survey at Duke University Libraries (Emily Daly, Duke University)
- Case Study 4.4 Listening to the student voice at Library and Learning

Services at Kingston University (Davina Omar and Simon Collins, Kingston University).

The University of Washington (UW) Libraries has a strong history of applying library assessment techniques to improve its service to customers. This forms part of the long-standing culture of assessment at the library, using evidence to shape and inform strategic developments. In Case Study 4.1 Belanger and colleagues discuss the large triennial survey used at UW Libraries since 1992, which has led to an evidence-driven culture of continual improvement. In providing examples of how librarians can act on survey results and how internal improvements in the assessment process can enable more effective use of results, the authors aim to provide librarians with ideas they can apply to their own surveys and service improvement efforts.

In Case Study 4.2 Sanches from Lisbon University also emphasises the importance of encouraging a continual improvement culture. She describes how regular assessment, analysis, action and evaluation have led to improvements in library customer satisfaction in key areas. Changes in the physical environment, collection management and promotion, library training provision and strategic planning have all been implemented based on the feedback received from surveys, to the benefit of the customer.

Duke University Libraries took the decision to move from using a standardised tool to developing an in-house library survey, as presented by Daly in Case Study 4.3. Following the lessons learned in their survey's first iteration, library staff sought to improve the response rate when running the survey for the second time. Following expertise from the Duke Center for Advanced Hindsight, they implemented a regret lottery method, increasing their responses from 733 to 3,467.

We have found few examples of in-house academic library surveys in the UK. One reason for this is the institutional desire for students to complete the compulsory National Student Survey (NSS; www.thestudentsurvey.com/) and to avoid 'over-surveying' students. Despite this, Kingston University has run an in-house survey annually since 2004, which has helped to establish a continual improvement culture and student satisfaction rise from 72% in 2004–5 to 94% in 2016–17. Case Study 4.4 by Omar and Collins provides insight into the use of a long-established in-house survey.

Survey design

The key strength of a locally designed survey over a standardised survey is the ability to explore local issues in depth. The essential starting point is to have a clear goal in mind for what you want to find out and how to use the information gleaned. If you are not willing or able to do anything with the results, do not embark on a survey.

Designing a survey and writing survey questions to gain insight into your customer needs and expectations requires advanced skills in qualitative and quantitative research methods. Depending on your institution, you may already have these skills within your library team; if not, bring in expertise to support you if you plan to develop your own survey. Seeking advice from survey administrative units or academic experts within the organisation, or even giving social science students a practical example that they could use in their assignments, could aid the development of your survey.

The growth of online survey tools has made large-scale locally designed surveys more obtainable and easier to administer. SurveyMonkey provides a free account for small-scale surveys or a reduced-cost professional account for students and academics. Before using SurveyMonkey seek advice from your institutional survey office as you need to consider data privacy issues (see below). Qualtrics (https://www.qualtrics.com/) and Jisc Online Surveys (previously known as Bristol Online Survey) provide similar functions to SurveyMonkey for a fee. In recent years these tools have become more prevalent and are often provided with an institutional licence; they overcome any privacy concerns as respondent data is stored locally rather than in cloud storage. These tools have similar characteristics allowing you to develop complex surveys with skip logic, multiple question formats, data analysis and reporting.

Before embarking on any survey, however, you must consider the ethics and data privacy issues raised. Many institutions have central administrative departments responsible for overseeing student data collection. In universities in the USA these are commonly known as an institutional review board; in the UK there is no standard naming convention but student survey steering groups, committees and/or departments are common and should be consulted. Local survey administrators have a responsibility to ensure that data is managed ethically and in adherence with privacy laws. Depending on the nature of the information collected and where it is stored, you may need to comply with the Swiss–US Privacy Shield Framework or EU–US Privacy Shield Framework. Again, your local survey administration unit, research ethics board or committee will be able to advise you.

Survey implementation

Once you have designed your survey in line with your strategic aims, it is vital to distribute it effectively to gain an appropriate response. For large-scale surveys e-mail is the preferred route of distribution, with follow-up e-mails sent at regular intervals until the survey closes. Incentives can increase response rates, and as Daly outlines in Case Study 4.3, 'regret lottery' messaging can be effective. Any incentives offered should be proportional and in line with the organisational culture. Providing a prize draw to win a round-the-world cruise would be seen as disproportionate, especially in times of increasing student tuition fees and institutional budget cuts. Sometimes less is more, with chocolate, a free coffee or print credits all being used effectively to boost student response rates. Promoting your survey in an eye-catching, engaging manner is also important. Like many universities, Kingston University has used a combination of social media, posters and online promotion and encouraging students and staff to promote the survey on its behalf (Case Study 4.4).

Survey analysis

The analysis stage of an in-house survey requires staff with appropriate skills in qualitative and quantitative analysis techniques to ensure data is evaluated appropriately. You or your team members may already have these skills, or you may need to invest in staff development or buy in specialist expertise, depending on your circumstances. Again, as with writing survey questions, you may be able to source expertise and support from faculty colleagues who specialise in data analysis.

Appropriate data analysis should be structured around the initial information need you identified before designing your survey. What is it you need to ascertain? How will the data answer this question? Who is the audience and what do they need to know? Framing your analysis to focus on the identified strategic needs will ensure that you do not spend time analysing data with little or no value.

Software used for quantitative analysis has been dominated by Microsoft Excel for years. The common use of this package for a variety of business functions has led to relatively mature skillsets in its capabilities among library staff members. With appropriate skill levels, it is possible to conduct analysis suitable for most in-house survey needs. Online survey providers such as SurveyMonkey have in-built sophisticated quantitative analysis tools allowing you to analyse the data within the platform. Within the interface weighted means, cross tabulations, survey comparisons and data graphing can be achieved quickly. All of the providers allow data export into Excel to enable further analysis.

In recent years data visualisation has evolved, with data dashboards becoming increasingly common. Tableau, SAS (formerly Statistical Analysis System) and Microsoft Power BI are all becoming prevalent, and examples are outlined in some of the case studies below. Tableau is used increasingly because of its ability to combine data sets quickly and create customisable data dashboards. Tableau Public enables you to use the product for free, but you need to be aware that all data sets are available to anyone, so this would not be suitable for sensitive data. If your institution has a licensed version of Tableau, data can be stored and shared securely, with a free reader version available to enable all staff to access your visualisations. The power of data visualisation to explore data in new ways provides us with more opportunities to answer research questions.

For qualitative analysis, similar software tools can support detailed evaluation of the data. In a later chapter on qualitative research we discuss the use of NVivo in developing a customer feedback database. This and similar tools allow staff to analyse, tag, code and identify connections in unstructured data. Qualtrics and SurveyMonkey also contain text analysis features within their platforms to enable analysis of qualitative data. These are not as sophisticated as advanced software such as NVivo, but depending on the information needed and the investment required in learning how to use qualitative software, they may be a better alternative. Regardless of the product chosen, the time required to conduct qualitative analysis can be significant, even for small-scale surveys, and should be factored into the planning process.

Survey action

The final stage of implementing an in-house library survey is action planning for change. This could involve stakeholders from across the library service or institution, or externally depending on the focus of your research. Identifying what actions need to be taken, by whom and when is crucial to this process. It is vital that you communicate your results to stakeholders who can help you formulate an action plan in a manner that is suitable to the audience. Sharing insight in an engaging way without overwhelming team members with data that is too detailed is essential to the action planning process. Actions could include lobbying for increased funds to improve library collections, space and/or services; redistributing resources to improve aspects of the service the customers care about the most; or improving workflows, policies or processes.

Beyond sharing your results with the stakeholders engaged in action planning, it is also essential to communicate your findings and subsequent action plans to wider audiences such as senior administrators within your institution, faculty colleagues and library customers. Closing the feedback loop by communicating findings and actions to the survey participants is fundamental. Ensuring that respondents are aware that their views have been heard and will be acted on will build trust in the service and encourage continued participation in future research projects. Sometimes this will include sharing with customers the news that their suggestions cannot be actioned at this time. There is often a reticence to disclose to customers what might be viewed as bad news, but giving bad news builds more trust and goodwill than ignoring customer concerns, especially if you are able to explain the barriers to implementing their suggestions.

Once your data has been collected, your analysis completed, your actions actioned and your findings shared, it is time to repeat the process. It is essential to check if the actions you have put in place have had the impact on the customers that you anticipated. Follow-up evaluations may not necessarily take the form of another survey; choose the right methodology depending on your information needs. This will then form the basis of your continual improvement culture.

Case Study 4.1   Beyond answering questions: designing actionable surveys to guide assessment, make decisions and support ongoing analysis at the University of Washington
Jackie Belanger, Maggie Faber and Steve Hiller

Introduction and background

This case study highlights key improvements made at the University of Washington (UW) Libraries as a result of quantitative and qualitative data collected through a large-scale user survey. In addition to discussing the concrete improvements arising out of survey results, the authors explore the ways in which changes to the process of developing the survey and communicating its results strengthened staff buy-in and willingness to act on the data.

The UW is a large, comprehensive research university with a main campus located in Seattle, Washington, and two smaller branch campuses within the metropolitan region. The UW ranks in the top three US public universities in external research funding (US$1.3 billion in 2017–18) with internationally recognised research programmes in the health sciences, global studies and science, technology, engineering and maths (STEM) disciplines. In 2017 the UW was rated as one of the top 25 research universities in the world by the Times of London (Times Higher Education, 2017) and the Academic Rankings of World Universities (Shanghai Ranking Consultancy, 2018). In 2017, student enrolment at the three campuses was approximately 42,000 undergraduates and 16,000 graduate and professional students. UW Libraries includes 16 libraries across the three campuses with a staff of more than 400 and an annual budget of $45 million. The UW Libraries is consistently ranked in the top ten US publicly funded academic research libraries by the Association of Research Libraries (ARL; www.arl.org) (ARL, 2018).

UW Libraries has run a large-scale user survey every three years since 1992, and the Triennial Survey, as it came to be known, is the longest-running cyclical survey in US academic libraries (Hiller and Belanger, 2016). It is distributed to all faculty and graduate students at all three campuses, to all undergraduates at the smaller Bothell and Tacoma campuses, and to a sample of 5,000 undergraduate students at the Seattle campus. Survey instruments and results (including dashboards and details about response rates) are available on the UW Libraries assessment website (www.lib.washington.edu/assessment/surveys/triennial). For additional background on the Triennial Survey and assessment at the UW Libraries see Hiller and Wright (2014) and Hiller and Belanger (2016).

Results from the Triennial Survey are used to make improvements to spaces, services and resources, and for budget and advocacy purposes. One of the challenges of moving from results to meaningful action in such a large system is that while library assessment staff (who currently include the director of assessment and planning, an assessment librarian, and a temporary data visualisation and analysis librarian) can gather and communicate survey data, it is largely the responsibility of staff in specific units to implement changes based on the results. Assessment staff are continually considering how they can enable staff to make improvements by gathering the best data and helping them work with the data in the most effective ways possible.

Survey development and communicating results

Before discussing the improvements themselves, it is worth pausing to provide some background on the changes to the 2016 survey and the process of survey development and implementation that enabled many of these improvements to take place. One of the major changes in 2016 involved a shift in the focus of conversations with library staff during the survey development process, which has always involved a lengthy consultation period with library staff, and discussions occasionally centred on the survey itself and whether various groups would see their concerns reflected in the survey. In 2016, the assessment librarian and the director of assessment and planning reframed their discussions with library staff by asking broader questions about what staff wanted to know about library users. Removing the constraint of focusing on the survey instrument allowed staff to generate a range of questions about users. These were brought to an appointed survey development committee, which worked with assessment staff to determine which questions might be best suited to survey methodology. The questions that were not appropriate for a survey were then used to inform plans for assessment in 2017–18. This enabled the assessment librarian to gather creative ideas for the survey that were genuinely rooted in staff needs and communicate to staff that any questions that were not addressed on the survey could still be part of other projects using methods such as interviews and focus groups.

As a result of this revised process, there were new questions on the survey that provided more concretely actionable data for staff (e.g. on electronic books, users' preferences for various search tools, and libraries' support for teaching and learning). Survey questions were closely aligned with libraries' strategic priorities between 2014 and 2017 in key areas such as scholarly communication. This alignment and the overall revised process were critical for generating increased buy-in from staff when they began to explore survey results and consider how to make improvements accordingly. While the UW Libraries has a strong track record of using results for improvement, the 2016 iteration further tightened the link and the timeline between the survey development process and taking action on results.

Figure 4.1 shows how we integrated the survey design process with annual planning and communication procedures. Depending on the stage of the process, stakeholder groups are asked about questions they have about users or those they would like to explore further from the results, which are used to inform follow-up assessment projects.

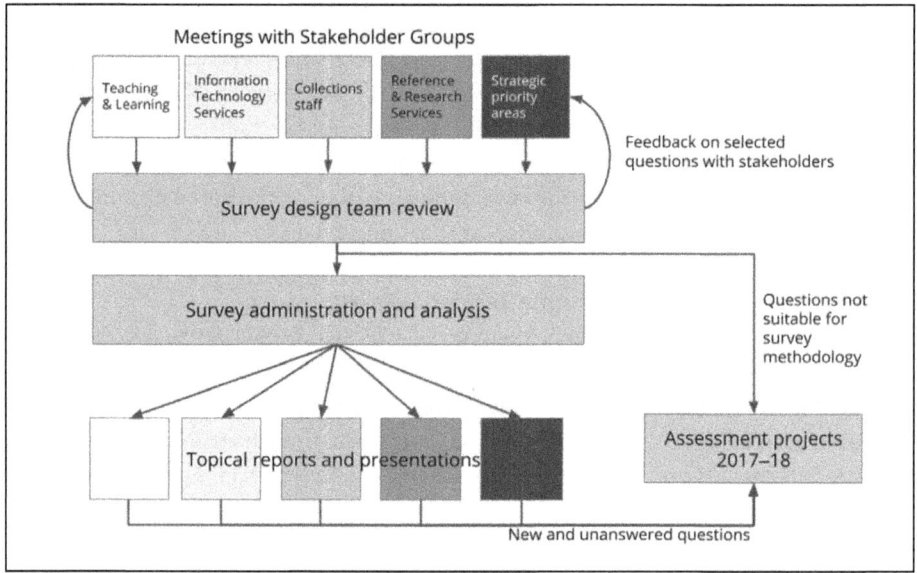

Figure 4.1 *The integration of the survey design process with annual planning and communication at UW Libraries*

Several revisions were made to the process of communicating survey results to libraries staff. In previous years, survey data had been made available to staff largely in the form of reports focused on campuses and major user groups (e.g. faculty). In 2016, assessment staff decided to create more customised, topic-specific reports for key stakeholder groups. They provided stakeholder groups with a detailed understanding of the results that mattered most to them, thereby increasing the likelihood that staff would be willing to act on those results. As a complement to the static reports, the data visualisation and analysis librarian developed a suite of interactive dashboards, which helped staff explore relevant results in greater detail and compare patterns across groups (Figure 4.2 opposite). In making the qualitative and quantitative results more accessible, these dashboards attempted to empower staff to act on survey results themselves. These various reporting models opened up new ways for units to integrate the survey results into ongoing service reviews and further assessment plans.

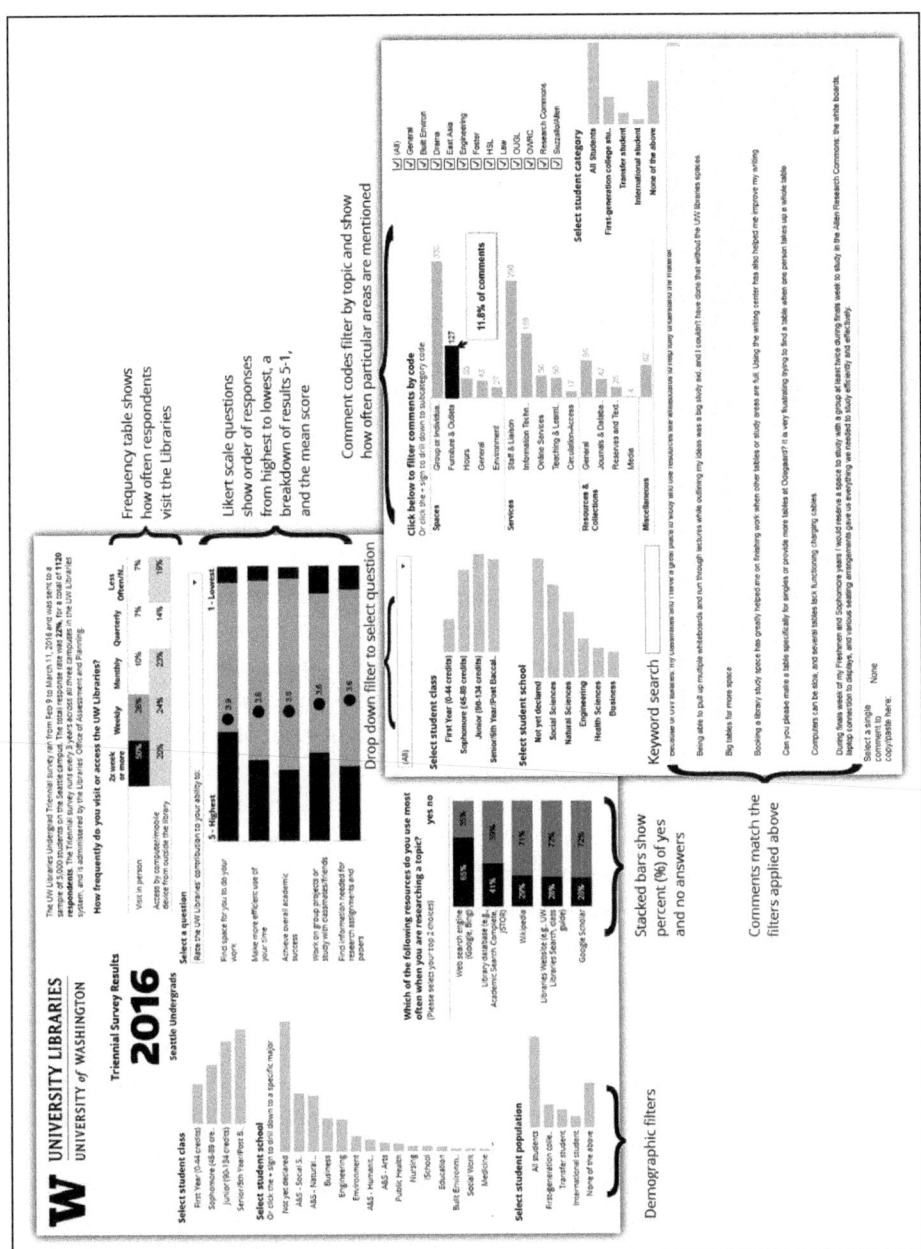

Figure 4.2 *Undergraduate dashboards from the 2016 Triennial Survey*

The dashboard in the upper left of Figure 4.2 shows the quantitative data, while the dashboard in the lower right shows the qualitative comments. Both are interactive and can be filtered to show answers from a particular subset of users or answers on a particular topic or service.

Acting on survey results

Data from the 2016 Triennial Survey has resulted in a number of service improvements. In all cases, changes arose after assessment staff provided survey data and comments to specific stakeholder groups, who then acted on the results. This model was key in ensuring that staff who best understood their own areas of user support had the data to make robust decisions about service changes. One key example arose in survey responses from undergraduates about the need for electrical outlets and space to charge personal electronic devices. A Likert scale question asked students to rate the importance of various spaces and the technology within them. Outlets emerged as one of the most important categories, receiving a mean score of 4.4 on a 5-point scale. The number of students requesting additional outlets was so high (about 24% of undergraduates' comments on library spaces and about 12% of their comments overall) that it was assigned its own comment code. As a result a number of libraries, including Odegaard Undergraduate Library, made a successful funding request for additional charging stations in the libraries.

Beyond using quantitative data from the surveys to demonstrate the demand for making particular improvements there are a number of examples of staff acting on qualitative survey data to change collection policies and spaces. For example, comments from students on the challenges they faced in accessing and using e-books re-enforced to library collections staff the need to improve access to locked content, which they had often encountered in person. As a result, collections staff decided to prioritise digital rights management (DRM)-free subscriptions to reduce access limitations and other restrictions on e-books. This decision prompted a cancellation of a pilot subscription with one platform in order to reallocate funds to another, and collections staff routinely now consider whether a resource is DRM-free as part of their ongoing decision-making process.

A number of faculty comments about fines on overdue library materials resulted in recommendations for service improvement. As part of a wider review, members of the Access Services Committee explored survey data and comments, focusing on users' criticisms such as the imposition of fines on the faculty. They noted that respondents had often commented on how UW fine policies compared unfavourably with those at other research institutions and investigated fines policies at peer institutions, resulting in them recommending that overdue fees for renewable items should be eliminated. Student feedback about library spaces also gave rise to improvements. For example, graduate students' comments about furniture and cleanliness at one of the UW Libraries were shared with the appropriate facilities department. Together, libraries and facilities staff identified low-cost upgrades to furniture that would refresh some of the spaces and agreed on a more frequent maintenance schedule for areas such as high-use study rooms.

These more focused instances of improvement operate in tandem with library-wide use of survey data. One of the most important of these is in the libraries' institutional budget request, in which survey results are used to highlight critical areas such as the ongoing importance of collections funding and key staff positions to support emerging areas of need such as scholarly communication. Over the course of 2017, survey results were also used as the basis for marketing efforts in order to ensure that users are aware of the range of library services, resources and spaces available to them and the changes made by the libraries in response to their feedback. Survey results formed the basis for more detailed follow-up assessments and ongoing improvements as well. For example, follow-up assessments using design thinking are being used to generate options for changes based on users' needs identified in survey results (such as a project to improve citation management support services) or to explore unexpected results in greater depth.

Conclusion

Although surveys are a popular assessment method in libraries, it can be challenging to move from data to action, especially in larger library systems. The changes implemented at the UW Libraries during the 2016 iteration of the Triennial Survey were critical in supporting staff to make improvements based on survey results. Changes include a revised process for gathering staff input during survey development and a greater emphasis on enabling staff to work with the results most useful to their areas of focus through customised reports and dashboards. The authors believe such approaches can be scalable in different library contexts, depending on the size of the library and resources available. For example, while creating a number of different dashboards might not be possible for all libraries, creating a customisable template to use for a variety of topic-specific reports can be a sustainable method of communicating effectively. Although time consuming, investing effort in gaining staff buy-in during the survey development process and communicating results to staff in more targeted ways pays significant dividends by encouraging staff to engage with survey data and think about potential improvements for users.

Acknowledgements

The authors wish to acknowledge UW colleagues whose work was critical to implementing the 2016 Triennial Survey and subsequent actions on survey results: Chelle Batchelor, Karen Brooks, Jewel Evenson, Ann Gleason, Corey Murata, Heidi Nance, Denise Pan, Kirsten Spillum and Jennifer Ward.

Case Study 4.2 Taking users' opinions into account when managing an academic library: a decade in retrospect from Lisbon University
Tatiana Sanches

Introduction

The University of Lisbon is the biggest university in Portugal, with 18 schools (faculties and institutes) and around 50,000 students, 3,500 teachers and 2,500 staff. It is governed by values of intellectual freedom and respect for ethics, innovation and the development of society, democratic participation, and social and environmental responsibility. There are 22 academic libraries, organised by themes according to the education and research of each autonomous unit. Two of these schools, specialising in psychology and education, frame the present study. The mission of the Faculty of Psychology is to offer training and conduct research in psychology and cognitive science. Currently it has about 950 students. The Institute of Education, currently with about 900 students, is devoted to conducting research and teaching in education and training in Portugal. The Library in question previously supported a single institution, the Faculty of Psychology and Educational Sciences, until the two separate institutions, the Faculty of Psychology and the Institute of Education, were created in 2010.

The Library of the Faculty of Psychology and Institute of Education at Lisbon University is reader-focused and open to change and innovation. This spirit has been fostered over the years by a working culture based on management tools. Thus, it has been crucial to define a mission, produce regulations and build a solid working structure rooted in a strategic plan.

In 2007, the management board challenged the library staff to undergo a reflective review, which led to a systematic observation on the general environment, human resources, collections, services provided and equipment, material resources and spaces. The first diagnosis pointed straightaway to the need to create and implement a regular methodology to evaluate the quality of the Library. Although this evaluation had been carried out on other occasions, it had not been done systematically and therefore did not provide a comparative analysis that would allow intervention in more critical aspects. In fact, strategic planning and evaluation are not regular tasks and only have a real bearing when they change into processes that are capable of changing according to the agreed objectives, circumstances and accumulated experience (Fuentes, 1999). Thus, evaluation is warranted in view of the need constantly to improve the provision of services to users, so that services are more satisfactory, efficient and effective.

Listening to users

Apart from previous diagnostic studies, we instigated an evaluation of services, spaces and resources of the Library, to be carried out in a simple, regular manner in collaboration with users. We used a satisfaction scale from 1 (less satisfied) to 4 (more satisfied) to cover the areas of library services, asking questions on its document collection, customer service and the staff's relationship with users, users' autonomy and accessibility of resources, the physical environment or space available, and the extent to which respondents appreciated the Library in general. An extract of the survey is presented in Table 4.1.

Table 4.1 *Extract from the reader survey of the Library of the Faculty of Psychology and Institute of Education at Lisbon University*

PHYSICAL ENVIRONMENT	Level of satisfaction				
	I have no opinion	1	2	3	4
01. Cleanliness					
02. Temperature					
03. Lighting					
04. Furniture comfort					
05. Noise level					
06. Atmosphere and decoration					

The first survey took place in February 2008, when we sampled 10% of the total school population of 1,500 students, which was equivalent to about 150 surveys. This proportion of students surveyed remained consistent over the years. But in 2016 a major change was introduced in the way surveys are gathered: from that date they have been distributed online. This change led to a significant increase in the number of responses, with 211 surveys collected in 2016.

Analysing data and acting on the results

Data analysis confirmed our first impressions. Generally speaking, the survey results have revealed an 80% satisfaction rate regarding the quality of the library services. Reasons for such positive results may lie in the efforts of the team, management and users themselves to improve spaces and services for all, each one making a specific contribution. However, in some cases concrete data provided the impetus for change and evidence of its impact: the spaces, the collections and their promotion, information literacy training and strategic planning.

Changes in spaces

In 2008 the least positive results concerned the comfort of furniture. We concluded that the furniture for study and consulting documents had to be replaced. Besides the aesthetic aspect of having different types of furniture, other matters of ergonomics, comfort, safety and user-friendliness arose. Changing the furniture also led to global changes as we increased the number of study spaces. When we reopened the Library in January 2009, we waited expectantly for users' reactions. Initial comments were reassuring and very positive. But it was only when we formally analysed the data of the 2009 survey that we realised how much impact these changes had: the satisfaction rate for furniture comfort went from 69.75% to 88.5%, the biggest climb of that year. Our readers truly appreciated the way we invested in new furniture: they now had around 30 more seats, which were more comfortable (padded and ergonomic), individual electrical and web connections, and table lighting – all designed for their comfort during their research and study. Details of these changes are in Sanches (2010).

Changes in collections and their marketing

In 2011, the surveys on user satisfaction highlighted the need to promote the collections more, as there was a mere 64.75% satisfaction rate in this area. This led us to define a strategy that not only promoted the collections but addressed collection management as a whole. We sought to give greater visibility to the collections by improving the information we provided on them, diversifying our means of communication, and projecting a dynamic, professional image to our users. We did this by creating new leaflets describing our resources, mounting thematic exhibitions, requesting reading suggestions, publicising the historical collection, presenting new acquisitions, and introducing a quarterly newsletter, institutional web pages and a Facebook page. As a consequence of these changes and more consistent publicising of new acquisitions, the following year user satisfaction ratings on collection management rose to 73.55% and in 2013 to 76.35%. Since then we have invested in publicising digital collections and improving access to them, guiding users towards these resources. Sanches (2016) recently described the impact of diversifying the collections.

Changes in information literacy training offer

Over the years, the survey has enabled us to evidence students' perceptions of the importance of library training sessions on their academic success. In 2012 there was a 75.40% satisfaction rate with our 'training offer for readers'. During the year that followed we strove to improve our training, some sessions of which were fully booked. At the same time, the Library continued to provide training in the classroom context at the request of teachers. In 2013 satisfaction had risen to 80.79%. We feel this evaluation showed the consolidation of our training practices and staff's personal commitment to help users develop their skills in information literacy. Details are described in Sanches, Revez and Lopes (2015).

Changes in strategic planning

The Library has sought to maintain a versatile service and communicate with the academic community that it serves and is a part of. We understand and demonstrate our commitment to teaching, research and science by responding adequately to users' needs and expectations. The implementation of a strategic plan for the Library since 2012 allowed us to define a new vision, reorganised into projects. All the tasks developed thus far and new activities were reframed according to this vision. Team members were empowered as projects were assigned to co-ordinators while more effective ways of controlling and assessing work could be put into practice. Each project was related to the Library's intervention areas and determined actions to be developed, timelines, performance indicators and expected results, and its position regarding the Library's global strategy (Sanches, 2014). Clarifying how each task fitted in the global vision motivated and gave meaning to the pursuit of individual work. In qualitative terms our criteria were surpassed, with our customer service provision rated by users at around 90% every year since then.

Conclusions

It is important to stress that the systematic improvement of services is effective only when based on high quality assessment tools, whether surveys or other instruments, hence the crucial need to evaluate them regularly. On the other hand, this evaluation is all the more important and credible if it corresponds to real changes with a view to actually improving service performance. The data presented, and implementation of recommended measures, must be analysed comparatively in order to assess if there has been a change in users' perception of the quality of library services. We continue to strive to support research and teaching, seeking to meet our users' needs, and improving our individual performance and satisfaction, internal communication, working routines and, above all, user satisfaction.

In truth, even our worst ratings had an acceptable level of satisfaction. Nevertheless, we felt we could make proposals and recommendations for concrete action to improve this satisfaction rate and the quality of our services in specific areas. We did, and continue to do so.

Case Study 4.3 Giving students voice: a biennial user satisfaction survey at Duke University Libraries
Emily Daly

Background

Duke University is a relatively young institution, but is consistently highly ranked and considered a peer to other prestigious US research universities (Shanghai Ranking Consultancy, 2018). Duke has over 15,000 students, including approximately 6500 undergraduates and 8,700 graduate and professional students in fields including business, divinity, engineering, the environment, law, medicine, nursing and public policy. Duke has strong connections to the surrounding community of Durham, North Carolina, and is active internationally through the Duke–NUS Graduate Medical School in Singapore, Duke Kunshan University in China, and numerous research and education programmes across the globe. Duke's students and faculty take advantage of unique service-learning and research opportunities in Durham and around the world in order to advance the University's mission of using 'knowledge in service to society'.

The Duke University Libraries seek to support the University's mission by anticipating the needs of faculty, students, staff and members of the public. We provide convenient access to a broad range of digital information yet do not lose sight of our most basic commitment to preserve scholarship in print form. Library spaces are a hub of learning, teaching, research and collaboration. Six libraries form the Duke University Libraries, and separately administered libraries serve the schools of business, divinity, law and medicine. Together Duke's campus libraries form one of the nation's top ten private university library systems (ARL, 2018).

Duke University Libraries staff have long been committed to learning more about the evolving needs of researchers and then implementing innovative services, developing new collections and building new spaces in response to users' demonstrated interests. Like many libraries, staff have conducted multiple university-wide surveys in an attempt to learn more about researchers' perceptions of the services, spaces and collections available to them. We administered LibQUAL+ (https://www.libqual.org) in 2002, 2005 and 2007 and LibQUAL+ Lite in 2011 and were prepared to conduct another university-wide user survey in 2013.

In late 2012, assessment and user experience staff considered the possibility of administering a survey other than LibQUAL+. While we appreciated the potential for benchmarking and comparing results across libraries that also use the LibQUAL+ framework, we found that we never actually made use of this feature. Perhaps more importantly, we heard from respondents and librarians alike that they found the survey to be too long (prompting our shift to LibQUAL+ Lite in 2011), the question format difficult to understand and the results cumbersome to understand and analyse. It was time to consider an alternative. After reviewing numerous in-house and consortia surveys from academic research libraries across the country, we opted to design our own survey, as we knew this would allow us to incorporate extensive branching and Duke-specific answer choices. While assessment and user experience staff members were motivated by the customised options and answer choices of an in-house survey, we were even more excited that a locally designed survey would enable us to involve staff at every stage of the survey design and implementation. We hoped that Duke-specific survey data would enable staff to make service design changes and help set the direction of future projects. By engaging staff in the survey project from start to finish, we hoped staff would be more likely to use survey data to inform changes and improvements to library services they provide or oversee.

Survey design, take 2

Analysing the results of the 2012–13 survey of Duke University Libraries helped achieve the goal of learning more about users' experiences with the library and enabled us to make improvements based on what we learned. We also identified improvements we could make to the survey itself. For instance, the survey response rate was fairly low, especially among undergraduates. We were also concerned that the meanings of survey questions and answer choices were unclear to respondents, thereby undermining the validity of survey findings. In the 2015–16 survey cycle, we endeavoured to strengthen the validity of the survey instrument and reach a broader base of potential respondents. We were also able to focus our survey on a core group of users this time around. In 2013–14, we had included faculty, undergraduate students, graduate students, staff and the general public in our survey sample. Because we implemented the Local Faculty Survey of Ithaka S+R (www.sr.ithaka.org/) in fall 2015, we did not target faculty respondents in recruitment for our January 2016 user survey. We opted this time to focus recruitment efforts on undergraduate and graduate students. As we knew our respondents would primarily be students, we were able to focus our survey structure and questions on this population. Another change is that we shortened the 2016 survey considerably by reducing demographic questions. We bypassed this section entirely by recording a unique identifier for each survey respondent and then worked with Duke's Institutional Research Service to collect aggregate participant data, including respondents' academic programmes and majors or minors, year at Duke, sex, race and international status.

Overall, we found that the structure of our 2012–13 survey worked well, so we preserved the flow: we first asked users which library they visit most frequently or if they choose not to visit a library. It was particularly important to liaison librarians in the sciences to hear from our users who do not visit a physical library; we followed up by asking why they opt not to visit physical libraries. We then focused our core questions around particular services, collections and spaces we were most interested in learning about. We asked questions we felt would help us gather information about users and, more importantly, prompt us to imagine and prioritise possibilities for services, collections and spaces.

The next section gave respondents an opportunity to share what they view as most important to their teaching, research and learning. We then asked that they indicate their level of satisfaction with the services, collections and spaces provided by Duke Libraries. In 2016 respondents had an opportunity to tell us what services or resource they did not know were available through Duke Libraries (e.g. data visualisation services, streaming audio, digital maps).

Finally, we invited our respondents to share which library services or technologies would most enhance their experience using Duke University Libraries. Respondents could choose from options such as specialised study spaces and furniture, expanded data and visualisation services, and support and increased digital access to unique or rare materials, among others. Respondents were also invited to write in additional services or technologies they believe would enhance their library experience or list equipment they wish they could check out from the library. This particular question is a major reason we chose to invest time and resources to design our own survey: we wanted to hear from our community what programming and services they would like Duke Libraries to pursue in the future.

Our assessment analyst and consultant took the lead on building our home-grown survey in Qualtrics, a survey tool Duke licenses university-wide. This was done with input from numerous library staff, potential survey respondents, and university staff and faculty with expertise in survey design. Using our 2013 survey as a starting point for format and question terminology, assessment and user experience staff led numerous meetings to refine the structure and update the text used in 2013. These changes reflected the resources and services we were most interested in learning more about during this cycle and ensured that question and answer options made sense to our more focused group of student respondents. In addition to leading small group discussions about the format and structure of our survey and questions, we shared our survey with all library staff at library-wide meetings and through e-mail. We wanted no library staff member to feel excluded from the process or be taken by surprise that we were leading this effort.

After weeks of discussion and work in Qualtrics, we had an instrument ready to test and then implement. Our final survey was short, taking users just four to six minutes to complete, but it was complex, featuring extensive branching and customised survey options for each of our library locations (Duke University Libraries, 2016).

Recruiting respondents

Once we had fully tested and vetted our survey with numerous students and library staff, we began to recruit respondents. Duke University's Institutional Research Office provided a sample of 5,889 undergraduates and graduate students. We directly e-mailed an invitation to these students to take the survey and followed up with reminders twice during the three-week survey window. Additionally, we posted links to the survey on the Duke Libraries home page and promoted it through social media, student listservs and subject librarians' departmental e-mails.

At the advice of a university expert in survey design, we opted not to provide incentives for survey respondents during the first implementation of our in-house survey. Because we were disappointed with our overall response rate in 2012–13, however, we decided to provide an incentive of a raffle for a $75 Amazon gift card this time around. Additionally, we worked with the Duke Center for Advanced Hindsight, led by behavioural economist Professor Dan Ariely, to develop a regret lottery (Ariely, 2012). A regret lottery is based on the notion that respondents feel more pain or loss if they believe they were very close to avoiding loss. We developed a survey invitation invoking the idea that students' names could be picked from the raffle for an Amazon gift card – but they could only claim the prize if they actually completed the survey. Our message included the following language: 'Your name has been entered in a drawing for a $75 Amazon gift certificate. . . . If you are the winner of the gift certificate but you have not completed the survey, you are not eligible to receive the $75 Amazon gift certificate.' On day one of survey distribution, we sent half of our potential respondents this regret lottery message; the other half received a more traditional survey recruitment e-mail: 'To thank you for your participation, you will be entered in a raffle to win a $75 Amazon gift certificate.' This split approach is known as A/B testing.

In the first 24 hours that our survey was open we received 1,200 responses, nearly all from the survey links we e-mailed directly to students through Qualtrics (four respondents completed the survey by accessing an open link on the Duke Libraries website during this same 24-hour period). Of the responses from the A/B testing, we had twice as many responses from students who received the regret lottery e-mail than from those who received the more traditional message. Within the first hour of sending the survey directly to students, we had 2.5 times more responses from those who received the regret lottery message. The response rate then normalised a bit over the first 24 hours. Because the regret lottery was so effective, we used the regret lottery text in our two reminder messages to all students who had not yet taken the survey. Our overall response rate from our initial sample was 43%, and we had an additional 945 responses to the survey through open URLs, resulting in a total of 3,467 respondents, significantly more than the 733 responses to our first in-house survey.

Analysing and sharing results

Because our primary motivation for designing and implementing a survey entirely in-house was to involve our colleagues in reviewing and responding to findings, it was important that we share initial findings as soon after the close of the survey as possible. After sharing high-level findings with library staff, we formed a short-term team of six library staff who volunteered to review and tag over 1,200 free-response comments using a codebook with nearly 50 different topics.

While we were able to gather useful feedback through the survey and free-response comments, we planned from the start to follow our survey period with a series of focus groups to dig more deeply into survey responses. After spending time reviewing the survey data, we hosted six follow-up focus groups, targeting undergraduate and graduate students to learn more about our researchers' experiences with particular services, collections and spaces they commented on in the survey. Just as we did when we designed the survey instrument, assessment and user experience staff solicited input from other library staff, this time to determine what we still needed to know from the initial survey.

By this point we had survey data from nearly 6,000 respondents, including over 1,200 coded comments, and notes and themes from six focus group sessions. It was time to share this rich data with our colleagues, which we did through presentations to all staff and follow-up e-mail. Additionally, our assessment analyst and consultant spent significant time using Tableau Public to develop three dashboards providing different ways to explore survey data and comments.

Making survey data visible and usable in so many ways enabled staff from across the libraries to analyse the data on their own. They could also ask assessment and user experience staff to help them delve more deeply into particular questions or slice the data by demographics particular to their areas. We encouraged units and departments to consider survey data and reflect on how library staff might respond to what we learned. We then invited all staff to participate in a workshop to explore the Tableau dashboards and prioritise an initial set of recommendations developed by assessment and user experience staff and departments heads of units across the libraries. There were 47 staff representing technical services, public services, IT, building services and library administration who registered to attend the session, working in small groups to explore areas of the data most relevant to their work or interests and consider ways they might respond to findings.

Responding to what we learned

After spending significant time exploring the survey data, comments and focus group findings, assessment and user experience and other library staff developed recommendations to follow up on what we learned. We outlined needs for further assessment, including developing targeted user surveys, semi-structured interviews and observation studies to learn more about researchers' experiences reserving group study rooms and using print and scanning services in the library. We drafted potential improvements to library spaces, services and resources. We also noted services and resources that respondents expressed interest in but appeared to be unaware of – these are marketing opportunities for library staff. In fact, we have established a monthly e-newsletter in response to multiple survey comments requesting more co-ordinated communication from the library. We have used the newsletter to share information about under-used services and improvements to our spaces. We will continue to use this channel to inform users of changes we have made as a result of student survey responses and focus group findings.

Library staff discussed and prioritised recommendations for expenditure, service improvements, marketing opportunities and assessment opportunities. Library leadership then charged task groups and other library staff to act on findings, and they have accomplished a great deal since the second survey. For instance, we have improved the libraries' interview rooms; added ergonomic furniture, including sit-stand desks and bicycle desks; and implemented new signage and wayfinding aids. Library staff worked with housekeeping staff to ensure public spaces and computers are clean, added troubleshooting signage to public printers, evaluated the effectiveness of the library locker programme, and made numerous enhancements to the Libraries' web interfaces.

Following the success of our first two in-house survey cycles, we will conduct another broad-based University-wide user survey in early 2018, this time targeting students and faculty. In the meantime, we continue to use the significant amount of data gathered from our 2016 survey, encouraging staff to explore the survey dashboards as they consider new services or the needs of particular user groups. We also support staff as they lead follow-up user studies and assessment to develop a deeper understanding of the many ways researchers engage Duke University Libraries' spaces, services, interfaces and collections.

Case Study 4.4 Listening to the student voice at Library and Learning Services at Kingston University

Davina Omar and Simon Collins

Kingston University is based in Kingston upon Thames in the UK, a busy riverside town on the borders of London and Surrey with just over 17,500 students. It has four campuses within three miles of each other. It has a long history originating from Kingston Technological Institute, which opened in 1899. In 1970 the College of Technology and Kingston College of Art merged to form Kingston Polytechnic with the Gipsy Hill College (education) merging with the Polytechnic in 1975. In 1992 the Polytechnic gained university status. It teaches students from over 140 countries a wide range of diverse subjects in business; science engineering and computing; arts and social sciences; art and design; and healthcare and has a wide research portfolio.

The university has a proud tradition of widening participation and has a large proportion of commuter students. Within this setting Library and Learning Services at Kingston University supports the students and staff in pursuing their learning, teaching and research ambitions. This is achieved by providing:

- four learning resource centres on each of the campuses
- generous opening hours at all sites throughout the year, including 24-hour access (term time) to the learning resource centres at Kingston Hill and Penrhyn Road campuses
- access to more than 350,000 books and audiovisual materials, 270,000 e-books and over 49,000 e-journals
- an archive including specialist collections
- more than 1,800 open access PCs
- subject support through academic engagement teams and dedicated subject librarians.

Student feedback is a powerful reason to drive strategy and Library and Learning Services at Kingston University has run an annual user survey since 2004. At the time the directorate had just been restructured and expanded to provide a more robust and enhanced service to the University. The service fitted the needs of a growing post-1992 university but the directorate still needed to know more about the students they were supporting and gather some forecasting data. Plus a previous survey in 2001 had given us an appetite to do more work in this area. At this stage the NSS did not exist and student feedback was not as prominent in the higher education sector, so there were limited other avenues to acquire this information. Therefore we decided to establish an annual library user survey with our students.

Methodologies

We investigated different methodologies and considered whether using a survey that would allow us to benchmark against comparator universities, such as LibQUAL+, would be advantageous. However, it was felt that having a survey that could be personalised would provide richer data and give us the opportunity to theme sections. This would allow for more detail to be discovered about a particular area which had been identified as a key priority for the service. It was important that we capture quantitative and qualitative data as part of the survey in order to enhance the variety of the data. Hearing students' own words can provide very powerful messages as verbatim statements can endorse trends shown in the quantitative data; they also give students the freedom to express their own ideas, which may previously have been unknown to the directorate. These factors continue to be an important rationale for running the survey 13 years on.

Initially the directorate used an external company that was very experienced in survey design. Over time, we took more responsibility for the survey, which allowed us to develop library staff skills in setting questions, running focus groups and conducting one-to-one interviews. This gave us increased resilience and ensured that library staff became more experienced in this increasingly developing area. It was also financially advantageous to the directorate. In 2010–11, we introduced SurveyMonkey (https://www.surveymonkey.co.uk), which allowed us more opportunities to cross tabulate and interrogate the data. We introduced a free-text comments question into the survey, allowing students to set out their priorities for the future. This generated more qualitative data than had previously been possible and had the advantage of students being able to supply a wider range of priority areas, though it led to significant numbers of requests for 'more computers' and 'more books'. These comments are useful for highlighting an area of concern but lack sufficient detail. One method used to combat this was to ask the students to categorise their comment first, into book, space, computer, etc., which encouraged them to write a more detailed comment. This worked a little better but we still have comments stating 'more'. Following university guidance in 2016–17, the survey has moved to Bristol Survey Online (https://www.onlinesurveys.ac.uk), a similar product to SurveyMonkey.

Design

There have been 124 different questions used in the survey over the past 13 years but some key questions have been included every year, which are kept static to enable trends to be evaluated over time and the use of key performance indicators (KPIs) for the directorate. For example, one of our KPIs is how many survey respondents agree with the statement 'Overall, the LRC [learning research centre] provides a good service'. Over 13 years the percentage agreeing has risen from 72% to 94%, which allows the directorate to demonstrate to the university that the service improvements and developments are having a positive impact on students' experience (Figure 4.3 opposite).

For the last nine years we have measured the proportion of students who prefer book format to e-book format. For most this period the preference for a print book has remained around 60%, but underneath this headline figure there were significant differences at subject level. In 2015–16, in the Faculty of Art, Design and Architecture, 74% of the students chose a print book compared with 51% in the Faculty of Science, Engineering and Computing. In the most recent survey, 2016–17, the headline figure has reduced to 42% choosing print book format, with 38% choosing e-book format and 20% choosing neither, which suggests we may have reached a tipping point in students' preferences. If responses in next year's survey show a continued decline in the number of students who prefer book to e-book, this will have an impact on the collection management policies we develop.

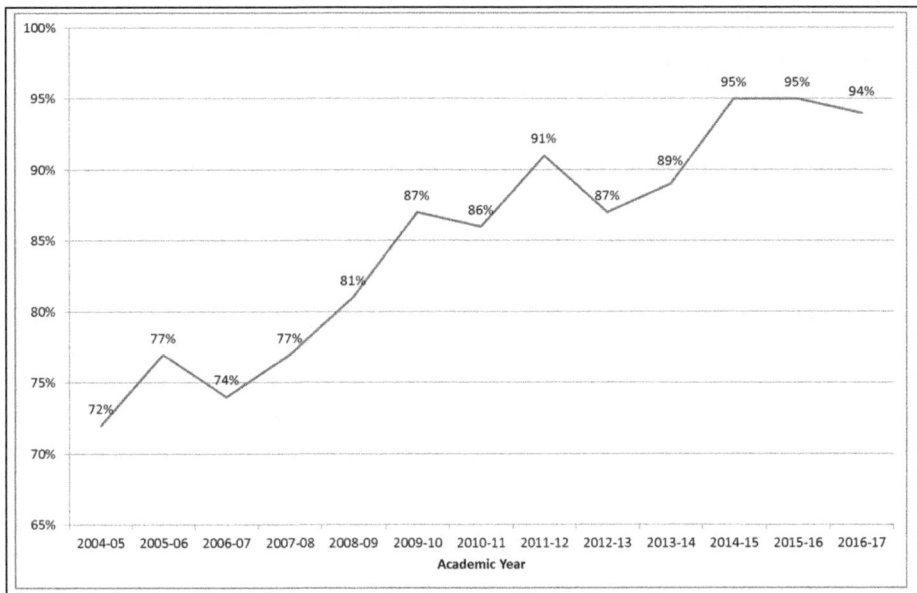

Figure 4.3 *The proportion of students at Kingston University who agree with the statement 'Overall the LRC provides a good service', 2004–5 to 2016–17*

Themes have been an important part of the survey and examples have included use of e-books, communication methods and use of computers. By having the capacity to ask four to five detailed questions on a topic, we are able to investigate the theme in depth.

We aim to have around 10% of the student population complete the survey – approximately 1,800 students. Although 10% is only a small proportion of overall student numbers, it is felt that this gives a large enough response rate to provide meaningful and worthwhile data. We track responses to the survey while it is running by subject and campus to ensure there is a proportional distribution. For subjects and campuses with low response rates, we focus on more additional marketing and promotion.

Marketing

Encouraging students to fill in any survey is challenging; we used a chocolate incentive which worked well. Alongside this there has always been a prize draw, which previously was for an iPad mini but most recently was a £100 Amazon voucher. Anecdotally, it is felt that the prize draw is not a major motivator in encouraging students to complete the survey and that most of them are genuinely willing to give their feedback once approached.

Library staff who actively encourage students to fill in the survey at stands in the learning resource centres and the help desks have a greater effect on the response rate than chocolate and the prize draw. The survey stands move between campuses' learning resource centres and are altered for the needs of the specific campus. The University has four campus learning resource centres of varying sizes. The stand is erected in the foyer of the two larger ones. Staff use tablets to ask students to complete the survey as they move in and out of the centres. Originally the stands had been staffed by a cross section of library staff but on evaluation we found that using learning resource centre assistants proved more effective, perhaps because they are students at the University and the peer-to-peer relationship works well. At the smaller sites, the learning resource centres are the social hub of the campus so there is less movement of students in and out. We are therefore more flexible in how we approach the students to complete the survey. The library staff also have a more personal relationship with students, which aids the likelihood of the students completing the survey.

In addition to promoting the survey within the learning resource centres, we put posters up in academic buildings, student offices and the Student Union, and advertise it via the virtual learning environment, intranet and plasma screens across the University (Figure 4.4). Student reps are contacted via e-mail and all academic staff are asked to promote it to their students. Instagram (https://www.instagram.com/ku_lrcs), Facebook (https://en-gb.facebook.com/KULRCs), blogs (https://blogs.kingston.ac.uk/seclibrary) and Twitter (https://twitter.com/ku_lrcs?lang=en) are used. It is not certain how effective these measures are in encouraging students to complete the survey but 15% of survey responses are submitted after the learning resource centre promotion is completed so we know they are having some impact. More evaluation work is needed in this area.

Figure 4.4 *Example of publicity for the learning resource centre user survey*

Analysis

The survey is analysed at University, faculty and department level using multiple demographics. Reports are produced and highlighted at University and faculty learning and teaching committees and shared at departmental student meetings. Actions from all the survey reports are pulled into a directorate action plan as well as departmental and faculty action plans. The directorate Student Voice Action Plan is an amalgamation of the survey actions and actions from the NSS and other feedback mechanisms. This has proved to be effective following previous separate plans and feeds directly into the directorate's planning document.

Every September, the directorate produces a leaflet called We Listened, which highlights the main results and actions from the previous academic year completing our feedback loop. Using individual students' comments, we explain how the action plan has addressed their needs on plasma screens across the university, on the intranet and in hard copy, taken to student meetings. This method of feedback is now used commonly across the University in a 'you said, we did' format as the University management thought we provided best practice in this area.

The survey data was invaluable in gaining and retaining the Customer Service Excellence (www.customerserviceexcellence.uk.com/) standard. The survey demonstrates our commitment to understanding our customers' desires, wants and needs, and understanding our customer segmentations also allows us to assist the University in its work on the student voice and experience. One such example for the future is the initiative investigating the attainment gap between black and minority ethnic (BME) and white students; we have nine years' worth of data on the library experiences of BME students that we can contribute to this initiative.

Challenges

There are a number of challenges with the survey including how to encourage non-users of the learning resource centres to complete it. We have tried several techniques to increase this number including taking the survey stand out of the learning resource centres, holding one-to-one interviews outside the main lecture theatres, working with the student reps and the Student Union, links within the virtual learning environment, and most recently within the Kingston University mobile app. These techniques have so far had limited results. Another challenge is that we have to be careful in the planning of the survey to ensure that we ask students to complete it at a different time from the NSS. The survey has been held at various times throughout the year but experience has shown that November to January is the optimal time. Students frequently comment that the survey is too long (35 questions in 2016–17), which presents a challenge, but it has proved difficult to reduce its length as the directorate requires certain pieces of data to be included and we need to analyse trends. To help reduce its size, we have run smaller focused questionnaires or focus groups for key customer groups – for example, postgraduates and assistive technology users. We also recently introduced ethnographic studies to complement the survey.

It is a challenge to manage over-surveying and survey fatigue relating to the NSS. However, University managers support us in running our own annual survey as well, as it yields rich data. This data also supports other directorates, in particular IT, due to the similarities in the services we provide, but also academic faculties, whose staff learn more about their students' interaction with academic sources. The longevity and maturity of the survey supports our case with the University, as we have a strong reputation for making changes to our services and resources based on the results. The survey has informed numerous developments and improvements made by the directorate including 24-hour opening, library design and layout, laptop loans, collection development, and the forthcoming landmark building incorporating a new library at the Penrhyn Road Campus.

Future changes

We generally score higher in our own survey satisfaction questions than for the NSS question on satisfaction with library provision. Further investigation is needed for why this occurs. In 2016–17 we matched the wording of NSS question on library provision in our survey. This will allow analysis on different demographics and year of study.

Conclusions

The survey throughout its history has informed the directorate of the way forward for its departmental plans and priorities. It has proved time and again a useful vehicle for articulating reasons for change, improving and developing services and, when appropriate, bidding for increased funding. It has also enabled the directorate to consider other methods of collecting data about our students – for example, customer journey mapping – as we understand the benefits of listening to students' concerns. University managers believe the directorate provides an example of good practice for our proactive approach and commitment to instigating change based on our findings. Our knowledge of our student population has increased significantly since 2004 and listening to the students is now embedded in our methods of working.

Conclusions

We have seen in this chapter how successfully developed and implemented in-house library surveys can help library service staff identify and implement actions that will improve customers' experience. Designing a survey to meet the strategic needs of the library can be difficult; question design and testing require skills. Similarly, data analysis and presentation are also complex. In-house surveys require significant time for design and implementation, but the reward of obtaining rich, library-focused data for action planning and change can justify the cost in staff time. As with any assessment activity, it is vital that you clearly identify your information needs and how the information will be actioned before commencing a survey with your customers.

References

Ariely, D. (2012) Regret, *The Dan Ariely Blog*, March 10.
http://danariely.com/2012/03/10/regret/.

ARL (2018) ARL Statistics, https://www.arlstatistics.org/analytics.

Duke University Libraries (2016) 2016 Student Survey,
https://library.duke.edu/about/depts/assessment-user-experience/student-survey.

Fuentes, J. J. (1999) *Evaluación de bibliotecas y centros de documentación e información*,
Trea.

Hiller, S. and Belanger, J. (2016) User Surveys at the University of Washington
Libraries. In Atkinson, J. (ed.), *Quality and the Academic Library: reviewing,
assessing and enhancing service provision*, 195–208, Chandos Publishing.

Hiller, S. and Wright, S. (2014) From User Needs to Organizational Performance:
twenty years of assessment at the University of Washington Libraries.
In Murphy, S. (ed.), *The Quality Infrastructure: measuring, analyzing, and
improving library services*, 1–24, American Library Association.

Sanches, T. (2010) Campus de Leitura: pensar o espaço da biblioteca universitária para
a leitura: o caso da biblioteca da FPCE-UL. In Calixto, J. A. (ed,), *II Conferência
internacional bibliotecas para a vida: bibliotecas e leitura*, 345–58, CIDEHUS/EU.
http://hdl.handle.net/10451/6605.

Sanches, T. (2014) Um plano estratégico para uma biblioteca dual: balanço da
experiência, resultados e reflexões, *11º Jornadas APDIS: As bibliotecas da saúde, que
futuro?*, 34–42, http://hdl.handle.net/10451/10970.

Sanches, T. (2016) Improving research and learning in higher education: digital
resources, e-books and a discovery system as enabling factors for students, *Journal
of Web Librarianship, Special Issue: International Voices*, **10**, 327–42,
http://dx.doi.org/10.1080/19322909.2016.1207583.

Sanches, T., Revez, J., Lopes, C. (2015) Sete anos de experiência, sete lições para o
futuro: formando utilizadores em literacia de informação, *12º Congresso Nacional
de Bibliotecários, Arquivistas e Documentalistas*.
www.bad.pt/publicacoes/index.php/congressosbad/article/view/1312.

Shanghai Ranking Consultancy (2018) ARWU World University Rankings 2017,
www.shanghairanking.com/ARWU2017.html.

Times Higher Education (2017) 'World University Rankings 2016–2017',
https://www.timeshighereducation.com/world-university-rankings/2017/
world-ranking.

Chapter 5

Library statistics

Chapter overview

There are two types of librarians, those who love statistics and those whose eyes glaze over at the sight of a spreadsheet. If you've made it to Chapter 5 of this text the chances are you fit into the former category. Libraries have a long history of data collection. Early records show that the Bodleian Library at the University of Oxford was collecting data on the number of readers in the 18th century (Thompson, 1951). Nowadays libraries collect a vast amount of data for a variety of purposes. In this chapter we explore some of these data sets and how they are used to improve the library service.

The following case studies are presented in this chapter:

- Case Study 5.1 Keeping purposeful intelligence: a case study from Learning Services at Edge Hill University (Helen Jamieson, Edge Hill University)
- Case Study 5.2 Assessing subject access in special collections at Harvard University (Emilie Hardman, Massachusetts Institute of Technology and Susan Pyzynski, Harvard University).

The wealth of data available frequently requires a library to develop and maintain a data inventory. In Case Study 5.1 Jamieson shows how various library data sets collected in the library can be used. The Management Information and Data Solutions (MIDAS) project team at Edge Hill University has worked with library staff to develop and understand data. By engaging stakeholders and building staff skills they have gone on to design key performance indicators (KPIs) which inform decision making and service planning, and advocate the service within the wider organisation and beyond.

In Case Study 5.2 by Hardman and Pyzynski we see how using library data to investigate the use of the special collections at Harvard University had an unexpected outcome. The initial research focused on using library analytics to identify which titles in the collection were most popular with customers. Staff wanted to evaluate which subject areas were consulted the most. Instead they found that items which did not have any subject-identifying metadata were used less than those with detailed records. Cataloguing practices in the past had focused only on recording item details, for example the title and author, but without subject headings. The belief was that users of special collections knew the item they wished to retrieve so subject headings were unnecessary. As special collections have become more accessible to a broader constituency over the last 25 years information retrieval practices have changed. The impact of this assessment has been on current cataloguing practices, which before this work were still based on the old beliefs and now include at least one subject heading for each record. Case study 5.2 shows how data can be used to inform process improvements to benefit customers of a library.

Overall, the possibilities with library statistics are endless, however your time may not be. It is important to focus efforts on obtaining statistics which can help you to improve the library, ensuring the data collected is put to work.

Collective statistical sets

Standardised statistic sets are commonplace and well established in academic libraries. Early library assessment focused heavily on output measures of extensiveness and efficiency as a proxy for quality and impact (Van House, Weil and McClure, 1990). Statistics from the Association of College and Research Libraries (ACRL) in the USA have been collected for over 100 years, providing a historic record of the development and trends in library collections and usage (Thompson, 1951). In Australia the Council of Australian University Libraries (CAUL) has published annual statistics since 1953 (Council of Australian University Librarians, 2018). In contrast, the UK and Ireland's Society of College, National and University Libraries (SCONUL) statistics were not developed until 1987 (Creaser, 2009). The chances are, if you are in an academic library you are going to be reporting statistics to at least one collective statistical survey, normally annually. Globally the International Federation of Library Associations and Institutions (IFLA) has compiled the Library Map of the World based on over 100 library data sets to provide reliable global library statistics (IFLA, 2018).

All of these statistical sets follow a common pattern of three key areas of data capture:

- expenditure and income
- collection size and composition
- library usage.

These are broken down into a variety of questions which meet the needs of the national body, although there may be some slight differences in the question wording between each of the data sets. As libraries and library services have evolved the data sets have developed with them, with statistics on e-book accesses and e-journal spend now commonplace. Results are available to members at an individual, sub-group or national level to enable benchmarking of service provision. Academic library staff spend a large amount of time completing the statistical surveys annually, but their usefulness in library assessment has been criticised (Loveday, 1988; Town, 2000). Disappointingly there is limited literature on how these statistical surveys have been used to improve library services and the call for case studies for this book did not result in any examples of current practice.

Operational library statistics

At a local level, libraries use statistics within their own institutions for a variety of purposes. Statistical data can be used to inform service design and efficiency, workplace planning, performance monitoring and advocacy. As previously discussed, with the volume of data available to help assessing library services it is often necessary to develop an inventory to identify, classify and manage the data sets available. This concept is explored in more detail below.

The common business concept of KPIs are described in the business texts within our libraries. These, often statistical, measures are aligned to the library strategy as an indicator of success in achieving articulated strategic aims. Carefully designed measures influence staff behaviour to ensure strategic goals are met. Writing successful KPIs can be challenging as it is important that they do not result in perverse behaviour or conflicting priorities. For example, a KPI that measures the increase in the number of helpdesk enquiries with librarians could discourage staff from creating any self-help materials the customer may need. A target to increase print book lending but not use of electronic information could lead staff to prioritise print book purchasing over providing electronic information. Successful KPIs support and influence library staff to deliver on their goals. Those attempting to embark on this process can find support in *Libraries and KPIs* (Appleton, 2017).

Operationally data is used to ensure successful service delivery and continual improvement. Across the library, data can be used to inform service planning, content management and workload planning. Within customer support departments, statistics can be captured on the number and nature of helpdesk enquiries to inform service improvements. This could include enquiries from students on specific topics or from the same course to help identify potential information literacy training requirements. Within collection management departments, data on the use and cost of collections is examined to support collection development and identify value for money issues. Library systems departments can use statistics to monitor web traffic and customers' use of certain tools and services to identify trends in behaviours. Recently the improvement of data visualisation tools has led to an increase in the use of dashboards for metrics within libraries to meet the reporting needs for these statistics.

Alongside regular monitoring, statistics are used by libraries for specific process improvements or research. This could include time-motion studies to identify the most efficient way to complete a routine task, for example processing an interlibrary loan. This business technique focuses on monitoring staff conducting the task, capturing all elements of the process and reporting the time taken for each element (Velasquez, 2013). The data is then reviewed to identify where efficiencies can be found.

Specific statistical research projects can also be conducted to investigate a current business issue or problem. Within an academic library context this could include a request from senior administrators to identify if purchasing library content in bundled deals represents good value for money, or how many customers have used a new service following a publicity campaign. As Hardman and Pyzynski discuss in Case Study 5.2, sometimes the findings of research projects can be unexpected, leading to unanticipated, but valuable, service improvements.

Statistics for advocacy

No library exists in a vacuum and it is important to communicate the value and impact the service has to the parent organisation. Service advocacy is vital to ensure decision makers and fund providers understand the benefits the library offers (Cook, 2017).

The use of statistics for library advocacy has previously focused on the concept of return on investment. This financial-based measurement of assessment in its original form takes the profit (gain minus investment) and divides it by the original investment to produce a return on investment ratio (Hernon, Dugan and

Matthews, 2014). In a non-profit context, for example a library, approaches to identifying 'profit' have included:

- purchase or exchange value, for example the retail cost to the individual to purchase the information directly from the supplier
- use value, for example the financial benefit gained by the user of the information provided by the library (Tenopir and King, 2007).

In 2013 the British Library produced a cost-benefit analysis report, updated from its original 2004 report, which found that the library delivers £5 in economic value for society for every £1 invested (Tessler, 2013). Within the local library context, tools such as the one provided by the National Network of Libraries of Medicine can be used to identify and report on cost-benefit analysis and return on investment (National Network of Libraries of Medicine, 2018). These methods should be used with care and consideration for the wider value of the library, which is not a purely financial relationship. There has been criticism in the literature of managers who focus exclusively on standardised statistics and return on investment as these measures are purely quantitative in outlook (Neal, 2011).

Case Study 5.1 Keeping purposeful intelligence: a case study from Learning Services at Edge Hill University
Helen Jamieson

Introduction
This case study will outline how staff at Learning Services at Edge Hill University have developed a set of key performance indicators (KPIs) to underpin our commitment to continually improving services, facilities and resources for all our customers (Edge Hill University, 2018). The case study moves from describing a project aimed at rationalising and prioritising the data we collect, to explaining how an original set of KPIs was developed and how we review the KPIs, data and measures to ensure they are fit for purpose.

Originally founded in 1885 Edge Hill, previously a college of higher education, is based on a stunning 160 acre campus in the North West of England. The campus has been ranked in the top three nationally for high quality facilities and voted in the top two for a good environment on campus by the Times Higher Education Student Experience Survey in 2016 (Minsky, 2016).

The mission of the University is to create and harness knowledge to deliver opportunity. In June 2017 Edge Hill University was awarded a gold rating in the Teaching Excellence Framework and was awarded University of the Year status by *Times Higher Education* in 2014–15. It has 15,220 students (HESA, 2016).

Learning Services is one of the largest academic support departments within Edge Hill University with approximately 130 staff based across 3 libraries. The department manages libraries, academic skills support, support for students with specific learning difficulties, media development, technology enhanced learning and the virtual learning environment. Learning Services has been a holder of the Customer Service Excellence (www. customerserviceexcellence.uk.com/) award (previously known as Charter Mark) since 2005 and has been awarded 19 compliance pluses over those 12 years.

Background

Our long-term goal at the start of the project was to use the vast amount of data that we gathered effectively, to inform decision making and service planning at all levels across the service. Given the diverse nature of our service we immediately recognised the scale of the task and so our starting point was to review, rationalise and prioritise the data we collected. A project group known as Management Information and Data Solutions (MIDAS) was set up with the following objectives:

- to define and create a shared understanding of what 'management information data' is within the context of the higher education sector
- to audit current practice for the collection of qualitative and quantitative management information within Learning Services
- to review stakeholders and their needs within the service, university-wide and externally
- to investigate good practice in the collection of management information and data
- to review systems and software available to assist in the collection of management information and data
- to make recommendations and find solutions for the future including raising staff awareness of the value and importance of information and data.

We carried out a process review of the current collection of management information and data within Learning Services, which revealed a variety of inconsistent practices. In some instances data collection formed part of an individual's role and was detailed in a list of their responsibilities. In others it was regarded as a function for a team and data was collected by a broad range of staff. Some statistics were kept locally on personal folders, others more centrally on a shared drive. In some cases we knew exactly why we collected specific data and what we used it for, in others we found we had been collecting data for years without using it to inform our service planning in any real way.

The MIDAS project took over two years to complete, and focused primarily on quantitative data. The project group made a number of recommendations around changes to the practice of data collection detailing what is collected and why, where it is stored, and how it is used and re-purposed. We made a significant recommendation on staff development, aiming to ensure all staff have a good awareness of the value of management information and how they can use the data for service improvements, storytelling and creating compelling narratives. We produced a roadmap for our staff which outlines where the responsibilities lie for the collection of data, how it is collected and the frequency with which the measures are reviewed.

Key performance indicators

Following this detailed review of management information and data across the service, and with a number of new processes embedded, we felt able to progress and develop a set of KPIs in an experiential project driven by a small working group, which reported back to the wider senior management team as it progressed. With no prior experience of using KPIs we began with more questions than answers:

- How do we define a KPI?
- Which data sets are true performance measures?
- How do we know that the data we gather is accurate and meaningful?
- How frequently should data be captured to ensure its value?
- How will we disseminate information to key stakeholders?
- How do we ensure the KPIs cover the range of services we offer?

We reviewed the literature but found little evidence of KPIs being used in higher education libraries, and when we found KPIs used outside the sector they predominantly focused on business or financial measures. Although it is common for library services to provide an annual report, or have a set of service standards, few had developed the type of KPIs that we were looking to introduce. From our research we concluded that any performance indicators identified should be directly aligned to our service's vision and values, strategic objectives, and the core values which underpin our local culture. After consulting our key stakeholders five KPIs emerged, each addressing an aspect of the service which underpins

Table 5.1 *Value statements and key performance indicators used by Learning Services at Edge Hill University*

Value Statements	Key Performance Indicators
Customer excellence: our product is high quality support and resources	KPI 1: Learning Services is the preferred place for study, support and resources
Operational excellence: our operational systems are customer focused and effective	KPI 2: Learning Services facilitates engagement with the learning and research environment
	KPI 3: Learning Services provides value for money.
Staff engagement: our staff drive our customer and operational excellence improvements	KPI 4: Staff are proud of the service and willing to go the extra mile
	KPI 5: Learning Services staff are engaged in customer liaison

our performance. The five KPIs sit under our three core values of customer service excellence, operational excellence and staff engagement. Each core value has its own value statement, which may seem under ambitious, but their success or otherwise is determined by the robustness of the measures and metrics which sit underneath.

The KPI on engagement with the learning and research environment was added because of our strategic developments around the increasingly important role of relationship management and advocacy.

Underpinning these KPIs are 33 sets of metrics and measures generated from activity across Learning Services and sometimes the wider university. They come from a range of sources including our own local data (MIDAS), our service standards, data from the National Student Survey (NSS), and wider university data. The KPI document includes space for 'intended direction of travel' (whether we envisage this particular metric increasing or decreasing) and 'value sought', which allows us to be more specific over the actual increase or decrease. For example, one of our metrics measures satisfaction with learning resources (taken from the NSS). Our current score is 4.35 (up from 4.26 in 2014–15 and 4.21 in 2013–14) and the value sought for 2016–17 is 4.37. Another metric, the percentage of staff reporting praise for a job well done in a university survey, is currently stable at 91% (the same figure as 2014–15) and up from 87% in 2013–14. While consistency of measures is useful when analysing longitudinal data and invaluable for spotting trends, the metrics and measures are not static and we will introduce (and remove) new measures if we feel the measure will add value to the KPI. For example, we recently included 'number of demand driven print and electronic purchases' and 'number of staff engaged in professional development programmes' as we felt these new metrics would promote our evolving service and the value we place on staff development.

Dissemination

We were keen from the start that our KPIs should be available for public consumption, but initially our priority was to ensure all staff across Learning Services understood why we had introduced KPIs and the value they bring. Team managers were briefed and members of the project team attended individual team meetings to discuss the importance of performance measures with other staff. As a result we have been able to achieve a high level of buy-in from staff. Collecting, analysing and managing the data needs investment of staff time and a number of individuals from across the service were given new responsibilities around data collection.

Our performance in relation to our service standards and KPIs features on our Learning Services web pages (Jamieson, 2017). On these web pages we publish our current performance indicators, how we have performed compared with the last academic year, and where we would like to be in the next academic year. Our KPIs feature in our annual report, which is also published on our web pages (Mackenzie, 2016).

We use the data we gather in a variety of ways:

- to measure performance
- in business cases to support new developments and services where we may need investment
- for our spring planning cycle (where we set out our objectives for the next 12–18 months)
- as a benchmarking tool
- in a number of projects where we have looked at the value and impact of the services we deliver.

In an effort to increase engagement with what can be quite dry data we have developed a selection of communication tools to market our performance in more engaging ways. We identified a number of staff from across the service who would benefit from staff development on interpreting the data into useful narratives to aid their promotion. We introduced the important role of storytelling and talked to key staff about how best to present these narratives using infographics and other data visualisation tools. We now use a range of methods to bring our performance to the attention of all key stakeholder groups online and face to face via attendance at faculty and programme boards and university-wide meetings. We also use the data in posters and social media campaigns; see example in Figure 5.1 on the next page.

Conclusions

Our approach to reviewing the information and data that exists in a complex library and information service has been a mix of strategic planning and serendipity and has developed over a number of years. We began with a focus on reviewing, rationalising and prioritising the data we collected and only then were we able to move on to develop our five service-wide KPIs and associated measures. We are aware that the performance measures and statistics referred to in this case study are largely derived from quantitative data that is sourced from across the service and University. When using this data for service planning we always triangulate the information with the wide range of qualitative data we harvest, including user experience work and the wide range of qualitative data we receive from university surveys and various customer feedback schemes.

Case Study 5.2   Assessing subject access in special collections at Harvard University
Emilie Hardman and Susan Pyzynski

Introduction

Houghton Library is the principal special collections repository of Harvard College Library. Its collections include over 500,000 books, more than 10 million manuscripts, and several million prints, photographs, objects and ephemera. Materials relating to American, English

Figure 5.1 *Example of a poster advertising Learning Services showing performance measures for 2015–16*

and continental history and literature comprise the bulk of these collections. We also hold special concentrations in poetry, and printing, graphic and performing arts. Houghton operates a busy reading room which fills with thousands of unique users every year from Harvard and around the world at every level of academic engagement from undergraduate to emeritus, as well as community members, artists and independent researchers. Historically Houghton was geared towards the service of Harvard faculty and graduate students, as well as non-Harvard affiliated scholars. In recent years, undergraduate students have become an important constituency for the Library, and programmatic investments in undergraduate students have led to a 20% increase in their use of the Houghton reading room. Classes held at the library have also doubled over the past ten years.

In September 2010 Houghton Library implemented Aeon, Atlas System's special collections circulation system (https://www.atlas-sys.com/aeon/). The system instantly allowed us to have more precise insight into many areas of operation and offered us the opportunity to routinise a number of data reporting and analysis activities. Further, the system amassed a large quantity of standardised data about the patterns of collection use by our researchers, facilitating assessment for areas of concern we were previously only able to understand anecdotally. Thinking about ways in which these data might open up collection use patterns for us, we began pursuing the question of what the subject headings of circulated materials might tell us about collection usage and research interests of patrons. We thought we'd find ways of looking with fresh eyes at the subjects represented in our circulating special collections. Perhaps, we thought, we'd find ways of challenging our sense of what concepts and areas of enquiry were engaged with in practice by our researchers. What we actually found challenged our cataloguing practices and opened up a new understanding of how our users may be exploring our collections and identifying materials for research.

Subject access and analysis

Our initial interest in analysing subject headings emerged because we thought it a useful way to put a user-centred framework around collections assessment work. We consider subject access to be a significant, if often insufficient, tool for access. From a pragmatic perspective, it is hard to imagine, at least with the tools and methods currently used for description, that we could ever even want to invest the time needed to provide anything like comprehensive subject access to our collections. Even the subjects of books, though bound in ways archives are not, may be difficult to describe fully. However, subjects and keywords offer users a way into materials that may otherwise not recommend themselves if only indexed by author and title.

The reasons users look for particular subjects, and the applications to which the materials they discover are put, are both broad and broadly unknowable. The subject headings of items which circulate are the most comprehensive means we have of examining a facet of our users' interests. Subject or keyword searching may be an early step in the research process and used by a less specialised research-oriented constituency, but they still may serve as important windows into the interests and research needs we seek to serve.

Subject librarians have analysed collections by subject and looked at other metrics or measures in order to weed collections (Mortimore, 2005), identifying areas that may no longer be of interest to users and removing materials from repository holdings. Subject analysis of collections has also been undertaken in the reverse: to identify areas for collection development, typically based on deficiencies in the collection (Bronicki et al., 2015). Subject analysis has been engaged with less in special collections. Our work in this regard is distinctly different from colleagues working with modern printed collections so our priorities and approaches to collection use are innately different. In special collections we must act with the understanding that a collection, book or piece of ephemera which is ignored for 50 years may serve as the foundation for significant scholarship in the future. We also know that in any given year only a very small portion of our collection will circulate. Recognising that what sits on the shelf is still important to us, we believe there is something special about what does circulate and in our quest to learn more about these items, subject headings can be useful.

Methodology and results

To get at the subject headings for the material that circulates from our collections, we first ran a report in Aeon, pulling up all unique circulation requests for September 2010 thru

December 2012. Unfortunately, about 15% of the circulation records were unusable because of missing bibliographic record numbers in the circulation request. Using the remaining 85% of records, and noting that our purpose was to look at patterns rather than frequencies, we removed duplicate bibliographic record numbers. We were left with 21,017 unique bibliographic record numbers for items circulated within our chosen time period.

We ran the numbers against our bibliographic database, using our bibliographic reporting tool Cognos Analytics (https://www.ibm.com/products/cognos-analytics). We output to Excel and parsed each of the 6XX subject fields. Once the data was cleaned, we ended up with 46,067 subject headings. Noting the variability in subject access on the records – some with a number of 6XX access points including Library of Congress subjects, as well as specialist genre terms, and some with nothing at all – we first wanted to see how many bibliographic records entirely lacked a subject access point. Examining the full list of bibliographic numbers we got from Aeon and comparing it to the list that produced the subject headings in our report we came up with 14,447 bibliographic records with subject headings and 6540 bibliographic records with none. Therefore 31% of the items circulated did not have subject headings.

We needed the context of our whole collection to understand this finding. Surprisingly, we found that out of 473,086 bibliographic records for the collection, 244,260 were without subject headings, so a majority, 52%, of our bibliographic records completely lacked subject access. This demonstrated that items with subject access were more likely to circulate than items without. Finally, we looked at the bibliographic records based on when we catalogued the material and discovered that items catalogued in the past ten years have a much higher percentage of subject headings and are circulating at a higher rate than other items in the collection. The fact that an item or collection is new may also contribute in a small way to its likelihood of it circulating, though the portion of the collection that circulates broadly represents the whole of Houghton's collecting history. This aside, this analysis of the data points to subject access as a key component for users in discovery and influences the likelihood that material will circulate.

Over time we have continued to observe circulation and note a consistency in this data throughout the three snapshots we have taken (Table 5.2).

Table 5.2 *Longitudinal analysis of circulation figures at Houghton Library, September 2010 to 2016*

Date of circulation analysis	Total records circulated	Circulated records without subject access	Records in collection without subject access
Sept 2010–12	21,017	31% (6540)	52%
2013–15	26,426	26% (6901)	51%
2016	12,126	28% (3352)	50.5%

Impact

When we undertook this circulation assessment we thought we would find new ways of understanding what interested our users in our collections from the meta-level of subject headings, but instead our analysis yielded a much broader finding: providing subject access seems likely to open up collection materials to discovery, and makes it more likely they will circulate. Such a discovery necessarily challenges the way we approach future cataloguing practice and look at our historical practices.

Through the 1990s it was Houghton policy that technical services staff did not prioritise the creation of subject headings for items in its collections. Near the end of his career in 1991, Rodney Dennis, then curator of manuscripts and manager of the technical services staff, gave an interview to the *Harvard Gazette* which illuminates the reason for this policy: 'I am persuaded, that something like 80 percent of the people who come to Houghton are coming to read and not to search for information. Our cataloguing is structured to accommodate that kind of reader so that we give them lots of access by names rather than by subject headings and things like that' (Dennis, 1991). This appears to have been a prevalent opinion among those managing 20th-century special collections, and ties in with views dominant at the end of the 20th century, manifested in the restrictions over who could use special collections and how.

Though our current professional landscape is one through which we have seen great strides in broadening access to special collections (Ress, 2015) and expanded notions of constituency for their use (Cook, 2015; Harris and Weller, 2012), a legacy of elitism is baked into many of our special collection and archive catalogues. This legacy presents us with some ongoing concerns regarding access, particularly for repositories with long histories. Archival silences (Carter, 2006), the evolution of subject heading terminology (Knowlton, 2005), and recognition of different information needs for our increasingly globalised user base (Chung and Yoon, 2015) have all been documented as issues for the profession, but the value-laden assumptions around collection use that have shaped our cataloguing practices still require consideration. In looking at our readers' use of the collection and the associated subject headings we have taken a step towards better understanding how we can align our legacy catalogue data with our current access values.

Practices and policies for cataloguing should move in step with our orientation to access. Certainly, there are time and effort trade-offs in supplying additional subject access to materials, but if access is a priority, such a calculation seems to favour the investment. Further, the expansion of our service to new constituencies introduces tension that may require some resolution. As we reach out and broaden our user base, it is important to consider how we can best meet the needs and anticipate discovery processes for users at many levels of familiarity with special collections and archives.

Even this initial work has informed our practice. It is now current practice at Houghton for cataloguers to assign at least one subject heading during the accessioning process. Since 2012, when only 48% of our holdings had subject headings, we have very slightly improved the proportion of our holdings with subject headings to 49.5% in 2016. It is a modest improvement, but one we can keep building on. Knowing that accessioned materials may not be catalogued until well into the future we may also endeavour to improve access by assigning more subject headings that appropriately represent our initial understanding of a collection's or book's contents. There is clear appeal in the possibility of assigning subject headings to the collection retrospectively, in order to improve the visibility of materials which currently lack subject access.

In addition to expanding our understanding of subject access and discoverability, we have also developed our assessment culture as a result of this work. The implementation of Aeon increased our available data and made it infinitely easier to query, offering the opportunity to ask new questions. We plan to explore this work further through user tests with a spin-off from our ArchivesSpace (http://archivesspace.org/) development site, which will be Harvard's primary archival discovery system in July 2018. With such a system we can establish a variety of subject access points for holdings and analyse the discovery process. As archivists wrestle with the best and most efficient means of applying their expertise to create optimal conditions for user discovery, understanding the parameters of subject access utility for users could be significant.

Conclusions

In this chapter we explored the helpful role statistics can play in library assessment and identified their limitations in assessing the library in a purely quantitative form. In later chapters we will explore the value and purpose of qualitative measurement. In order to fully assess a library and articulate its value a combination of qualitative and quantitative measurement must be used.

References

Appleton, L. (ed) (2017) *Libraries and Key Performance Indicators: a framework for practitioners*, Chandos Publishing, doi: https://doi.org/10.1016/C2014-0-03696-9.

Bronicki, J., Ke, I., Turner, C. and Vaillancourt, S. (2015) Gap Analysis by Subject Area of the University of Houston Main Campus Library Collection, *Serials Librarian*, **68**, 230–42.

Carter, R. S. (2006) Of Things Said and Unsaid: power, archival silences, and power in silence, *Archivaria*, **61**, 215–33.

Chung, E. K. and Yoon, J. W. (2015) An Exploratory Analysis of International Students' Information Needs and Uses, *Canadian Journal of Information & Library Sciences*, **39** (1), 36–59.

Cook, M. (2015) Build it and they will come: integrating unique collections and undergraduate research, *Collection Building*, **34** (4), 128–33.

Cook, C. (2017) Assessing Assessment in Libraries. Presented at the *12th International*

Conference on Performance Measurement in Libraries, Oxford, 2 August (unpublished).

Council of Australian University Librarians (2018) CAUL Statistics, https://statistics.caul.edu.au/.

Creaser, C. (2009) UK Higher Education Library Statistics. In Heaney, M. (ed.), *Library Statistics for the Twenty-First Century World*, Walter de Gruyter, 261–72, doi: https://doi.org/10.1515/9783598441677.4.261.

Dennis, R. (1991) Q&A: a conversation with Rodney Dennis, *Harvard Gazette*, 15 March.

Edge Hill University (2018) About Us, https://www.edgehill.ac.uk/ls/about/?tab=measuring-our-performance.

Harris, V. A. and Weller, A. C. (2012) Use of Special Collections as an Opportunity for Outreach in the Academic Library, *Journal of Library Administration*, **52**, 294–303.

Hernon, P., Dugan, R. E. and Matthews, J. R. (2014) *Getting Started with Evaluation*, American Library Association, http://ebookcentral.proquest.com/lib/open/detail.action?docID=1711154.

HESA (2016) Who's studying in HE?, https://www.hesa.ac.uk/data-and-analysis/students/whos-in-he

IFLA (2018) IFLA Map of the World: about, http://librarymap.ifla.org/about.

Jamieson, H. (2017) Learning Services Key Performance Indicators, www.edgehill.ac.uk/ls/about/measuring-our-performance/.

Knowlton, S. A. (2005) Three Decades Since 'Prejudices and Antipathies': a study of changes in the Library of Congress Subject Headings, *Cataloging & Classification Quarterly*, **40** (2), 123–45.

Loveday, A. J. (1988) Statistics for Management and Trend Analysis: a SCONUL experiment, *IFLA Journal*, **14** (4), 334–42, doi: 10.1177/034003528801400406.

Mackenzie, A. (2016) Learning Services Annual Report 2016, www.edgehill.ac.uk/ls/about/annual-report/.

Minsky, C. (2016) THE Student Experience Survey 2016 results, *Times Higher Education*, March 17, https://www.timeshighereducation.com/student/news/student-experience-survey-2016-results

Mortimore, J. M. (2005) Access-Informed Collection Development and the Academic Library: using holdings, circulation, and ILL data to develop prescient collections, *Collection Management*, **30** (3), 21–37.

National Network of Libraries of Medicine (2018) Cost Benefit and ROI Calculator, https://nnlm.gov/mcr/training/program-evaluation/cost-benefit-and-roi-calculator.

Neal, J. G. (2011) Stop the Madness: the insanity of ROI and the need for new qualitative measures of academic library success, *2011 ACRL Conference,* Association of College and Research Libraries, 424–9, www.ala.org/acrl/sites/ala.org.acrl/files/content/conferences/confsandpreconfs/nati onal/2011/papers/stop_the_madness.pdf.

Ress, S. (2015) Special Collections: improving access and usability, *Reference Librarian*, **56** (1), 52–8.

Tenopir, C. and King, D. W. (2007) Perceptions of Value and Value Beyond Perceptions: measuring the quality and value of journal article readings, *Serials*, **20**, 199–207, doi: 10.1629/20199.

Tessler, A. (2013) Economic Valuation of the British Library, www.bl.uk/aboutus/stratpolprog/increasingvalue/britishlibrary_ economicevaluation.pdf.

Thompson, L. S. (1951) History of the Measurement of Library Service, *Library Quarterly*, **21**, 94–106, doi: 10.1086/617755.

Town, J. S. (2000) Performance or Measurement?, *Performance Measurement and Metrics*, **1**, 43–54, doi: 10.1108/EUM0000000007224.

Van House, N. A., Weil, B. T. and McClure, C. R. (1990) *Measuring Academic Library Performance: a practical approach*, American Library Association.

Velasquez, D. L. (2013) *Library Management 101: a practical guide*, American Library Association, http://ebookcentral.proquest.com/lib/open/detail.action?docID=1672832.

Chapter 6

Qualitative feedback

Chapter overview

Academic libraries receive a huge amount of qualitative data about what customers want, and how they are performing. This might be explicitly sought via a survey as discussed in chapters two, three and four, or through qualitative research techniques, such as focus groups and interviews. Alternatively, it may be unsolicited via social media, a feedback book, a form on the library website, or simply from interactions with library staff. How can this data be harnessed to improve the library? How can the data be analysed? Should we make changes based on one person's opinion?

This chapter describes how libraries can get more from such feedback: by using it to answer future business questions; and through undertaking deeper analysis to gain insights. It also describes how to address some of the common challenges that arise when using qualitative data. Each area is illustrated by one of the three case studies:

- Case Study 6.1 Breaking out of the silos: taking the holistic view of customer feedback at Cranfield University (Selena Killick, Open University)
- Case Study 6.2 Digging deeper: using qualitative data analysis of survey feedback to inform library strategy at the University of Oxford (Frankie Wilson, University of Oxford)
- Case Study 6.3 Let the computer take the strain: automatic analysis of LibQUAL+ free-text comments at Singapore Management University Libraries (Tamera Hanken, Xavier University of Louisiana).

Using qualitative data to improve customers' experience

Libraries rarely need to employ a full qualitative research design, such as that espoused in the social science methodological literature (e.g. Denzin and Lincoln, 2005). Nor is it usually appropriate to apply true grounded theory techniques, such as those described by Anselm Strauss (e.g. Strauss and Corbin, 1998) to qualitative data analysis. Therefore, if someone who wishes to analyse their customer feedback trawls along the shelves in the qualitative methodology section of a library they are likely to conclude that it is too time consuming and complex. However, by applying the principles of such methods judiciously, qualitative feedback can be used to drive change without the risk of the library being accused that it is merely responding to those who shout the loudest.

Of course, some feedback can (and arguably should) lead directly to action – if a comment in a feedback book states that the lock on the toilet door is broken, and it is, that can be actioned immediately. If a tweet complains that the photocopiers always run out of paper by 4:30pm on Fridays, and it is observed to be true, this can be addressed by re-stocking them at 4pm. If a comment on the survey says that Professor X recommended such-and-such a book as essential for their course, and an e-mail to the professor confirms this, it can be purchased. These are examples where qualitative feedback has illuminated an issue that would have been addressed immediately if discovered by library staff. Addressing them certainly improves customers' experience, but qualitative feedback can work harder.

Case Study 6.1 describes how the first author of this book put such comments to work by developing a customer feedback database in her previous role at Cranfield University. The database brought together feedback comments from four surveys, and qualitative data from interviews and focus groups. This central knowledge base enabled staff to answer key business questions from existing data, without the need to undertake a fresh data gathering exercise each time.

The value of qualitative feedback does not end there. Further analysis can lead to novel insights about customers and so deep changes to library programmes, provision and strategy. The established method for distilling understanding and explanation from qualitative data is interpretative synthesis (Noblit and Hare, 1988). This approach is primarily concerned with the development of concepts, and theories that integrate those concepts, through induction and interpretation (Dixon-Woods et al., 2006).

Interpretative synthesis has two main phases (reading and annotating raw data, then coding and categorising the data) and a number of elements, but it does not follow a particular plan as the pathway is set by the data. Although all such analysis starts and ends at the same place, the route between the two is different every time, because of the different levels of iteration required by the data. An outline of the major aspects of the method is given below, and a selection of books that will lead you through the process in detail is listed in the section 'Further resources' at the end of this chapter.

All interpretative synthesis starts with reading and annotating the raw data. The goal of this initial phase is to remain open to all possible theoretical explanations for your reading of the data. Initial coding sticks very closely to the text and should be undertaken quickly after the data has been collected, in order to capture the initial thoughts that occur at this first view of the data. The size of unit of data coded depends on the research purpose and indeed the data itself. Traditional grounded theory (e.g. Strauss and Corbin, 1998) tends to recommend word-by-word coding. However, this very time-consuming approach is not appropriate for analysing customer feedback to determine how to make improvements. Lack of time may tempt you to undertake thematic analysis (as described above and illustrated in Case Study 6.1), which leads to useful understanding of the data, but is not sufficient for interpretative synthesis as crucial nuances and consequent ideas will escape your attention (Charmaz, 2013). A sensible middle ground is line-by-line coding, where every line of your data is given a code.

Following the initial phase, focused coding is used to identify and develop the most salient categories in the data, and start building an explanatory theory. The most significant or frequent codes are used to sort, integrate, synthesise and organise the data (Charmaz, 2013). This leads to hypotheses about how the salient codes relate to each other, which eventually becomes the theory (Glaser, 1992).

A crucial aspect of interpretative synthesis is the need for constant comparison. During the initial phase, data is compared with data to find similarities and differences. Then comparing examples of the same code encourages critical thinking about that code in order to ensure it reflects the data appropriately. As the analysis progresses, comparing new data with existing codes and new codes with existing data deepens understanding and tests the adequacy of the codes.

Another key feature is memo-writing. This is the process of capturing insights that arise as you move through the data and coding process. It prompts you to analyse your data and codes early in the analysis process, and helps increase the level of abstraction of your ideas (Charmaz, 2013).

The second case study, from this book's second author, illustrates how interpretative synthesis of survey feedback can lead to service improvements. Two areas of long-standing negative feedback were previously considered unresolvable, but analysis led to insight into the underlying reason for them both, and including actions to address this underlying issue in the Bodleian Libraries' strategic plan.

Challenges

There are a number of challenges in using qualitative data to improve customers' experience, two of which are described below, with some potential solutions.

Challenge 1: 'What is your sample size?'

As described in the much cited work by Orlikowski and Baroudi (1991), the quantitative paradigm is appropriate where quantifiable measures of variables are possible, where hypotheses can be formulated and tested, and inferences drawn from sample to populations. The qualitative paradigm is appropriate when the phenomena under study are complex and social in nature, and when understanding the cultural context from which people derive meaning is important. Qualitative and quantitative research are equal – different, but equal; quantitative is not the 'gold standard' and qualitative the runner up. Nevertheless, the vocabulary used to describe how to ensure that quantitative analysis is trustworthy is so ingrained that most people presented with qualitative findings question the reliability and validity of the results, usually by asking 'what is your sample size?' As Wolcott so acerbically put it, 'A discussion of validity [of qualitative research] signals a retreat to that pre-existing vocabulary originally designed to lend precision to one arena of dialogue and too casually assumed to be adequate for another' (1990, 168).

Lincoln and Guba (1985) described the four concepts used to determine the trustworthiness of research:

- *truth value*: confidence in the truth of the findings
- *applicability*: demonstration of how generalisable the results are outside the participants
- *consistency*: confidence that the results could be repeated
- *neutrality*: the extent to which the findings are shaped by the participants and not researcher bias or motivation.

Validity, reliability and objectivity are the methods of judging these aspects for quantitative data; for qualitative data the methods are credibility, transferability, dependability and confirmability (Table 6.1 opposite). We have gone into detail about this because the only solution to being asked about the sample size of your qualitative data is to explain that such concepts do not apply to qualitative research, and then explain how you have ensured your results are trustworthy using the standards for the paradigm (see the section 'Further resources' for a selection of guides).

Table 6.1 *Methods of judging value in research* (Pickard, 2013, 20)

	Quantitative methodology	Qualitative methodology	Mixed methods approach
Truth value	Internal validity	Credibility	Validity and credibility
Applicability	External validity	Transferability	Generalisability
Consistency	Reliability	Dependability	Synchronic reliability
Neutrality	Objectivity	Confirmability	Objectivity

Challenge 2: 'When will we get the results?'

Qualitative data analysis takes time. A great deal of time. At the very basic level, every comment must be read, and those illuminating 'quick wins' pulled out so they can be fixed. In addition, a simple tally of types of feedback is useful (e.g. 95% of comments were positive; half the comments were about noise, etc.), but this takes longer than simply reading them. The time needed for both of these tasks can be ameliorated by having a number of people undertake this work – there is no analysis so consistency is not an issue. Only minimal instructions are required.

Coding feedback comments takes time, to undertake the work and to prepare for it through training (Case Study 6.1). Consistency is important, so this needs to be undertaken by only a small team of people, who regularly repeat aspects of each other's coding (Charmaz, 2013).

Taking the final step into interpretative synthesis takes yet more time, and expertise (Case Study 6.2). Fortunately qualitative analysis, like most things, gets quicker with practice. It will still take much, much longer than quantitative data analysis, but never as long as the first time!

The third case study illustrates a potential solution to this challenge. In it, Hanken describe her use of text mining as a novel way of addressing this challenge. This collaboration between the Singapore Management University Library and the School of Information Systems created a computer program to automatically identify concepts, patterns and topics in the text of LibQUAL+ free-text comments.

Case Study 6.1 Breaking out of the silos: taking the holistic view of customer feedback at Cranfield University
Selena Killick

Background

Cranfield University is the UK's only wholly postgraduate university specialising in science, technology, engineering and management subjects. It is one of the top five research-intensive universities in the UK. Approximately 4,500 students study at the university every year, supported by around 1,500 staff members. Cranfield Libraries consist of three branch libraries, two at the Cranfield campus and one at the Shrivenham campus approximately 70 miles from Cranfield. The libraries strive to meet the needs of our community by providing information and library services at a level expected by our customers. We have a strong history of library assessment, with a culture of continuous improvement supported by performance measurement. Under the leadership of Stephen Town, we introduced the LibQUAL+ (www.libqual.org) survey to the UK higher education sector in 2003, piloting the methodology outside the USA for the first time. Following the successful pilot we included LibQUAL+ in our annual assessment programme.

Developing a customer feedback database

The customer feedback database at Cranfield Libraries developed organically after I conducted a customer needs analysis in 2011 (Killick, 2012). The research project set out to identify if the LibQUAL+ survey was still measuring what customers wanted from Cranfield Libraries. It comprised a series of focus groups with different types of customers who were asked to identify what they needed from library services. The aim at the time was not to focus on Cranfield specifically but to discover general requirements of academic libraries. All of the sessions were recorded, transcribed and analysed using the qualitative research software ATLAS.ti (https://atlasti.com). Applying a grounded theory approach, the transcripts were reviewed and coded until the common themes of customer needs could be identified. The research ultimately concluded that the LibQUAL+ methodology was still evaluating the key themes that mattered to our customers (Killick, 2012).

Six months after concluding the research, we commenced a review of the reference management software being provided on licence by Cranfield Libraries. Owing to changes in the marketplace and economic pressures, we felt that new free alternative products may provide better value for money for our customers. The project team needed to know what our customers' expectations of reference management software were and approached me to conduct some research into this area. As the previous research project into customers' expectations had explored reference management software, I already had the data they required. I was able to extract quickly and easily all comments that had been made on reference management software from the ATLAS.ti database. I analysed the findings and provided the team with an overview of customers' expectations in a fraction of the time research of this nature would normally take us. The project team used the information to make a customer-based informed decision about our future support for this service. The time and money saved from having to conduct a separate piece of primary research or analyse the previously collected data again led me to develop a new customer feedback management strategy.

The new customer feedback management strategy had five key aims:

- to maximise the value of customer feedback received by conducting regular, systematic analysis of all qualitative data

- to take a holistic approach to analysing qualitative data
- to bring all qualitative customer feedback into a centralised database, regardless of communication channel
- to provide an annual report on key customer feedback findings to inform strategic planning
- to provide an ad hoc feedback query service for all library staff to aid business decisions.

Like most libraries, we dedicated resources to reviewing the qualitative comments received from our customers via the LibQUAL+ survey and other communication channels when the feedback was captured. This analysis was conducted within the confines of the methodology applied at the time. Data received via one communication channel (e.g. the institutional satisfaction survey) was analysed, conclusions drawn, findings presented and the cycle was repeated. While this approach can work for specific research questions, wider learnings taken from a holistic long-term view were being missed. The findings also varied depending on the research methodology and questions posed. In the case of the LibQUAL+ qualitative comments, customers naturally commented on topics that had been presented in the survey. Owing to the standardised nature of the survey, however, our respondents rarely mentioned local issues, such as our wireless internet and the provision of computers. In contrast, the institutional satisfaction survey asked 'What, if anything, would you change about Cranfield's library services and why?' Feedback from this communication channel was dominated by comments about the IT infrastructure within the library.

Building a customer feedback database

Following my recommendations, the senior management team approved the development of a central customer feedback database, bringing all sources of qualitative feedback into a central knowledge base, which could be interrogated regardless of communication channel. Initially this included:

- LibQUAL+ free-text comments
- institutional satisfaction survey comments
- comments made about the library via the Postgraduate Taught Experience Survey (PTES) and Postgraduate Research Experience Survey (PRES)
- interview transcripts
- focus group transcripts.

With future plans to include:

- social media comments
- usability testing feedback

- customer complaints and compliments
- feedback on the library captured through academic quality reviews.

We purposely chose to exclude customer enquiries from the database. The library service had an established customer enquiry management system which included reporting functionality on the number and nature of enquiries received. We had also established a customer relationship management system to support relationship management with academic staff, research and other professional colleagues. The system is used to record discussions with academic staff regarding their research, teaching and library needs. Information on enquiries made, discussions held, courses taught, training attended, key journals and core databases are recorded for each customer. Again, as this system had existing reporting functionality, we decided to exclude this qualitative data from the customer feedback strategy.

The database built on the previous work already conducted in ATLAS.ti for the customer needs analysis research, but changes to the university provision of qualitative analysis software meant that it needed to be built in NVivo (www.qsrinternational.com/nvivo), a similar competing product. Thankfully it was possible to transfer the data analysis from one product to another without the need to re-analyse the qualitative data.

While the basics of NVivo are relatively straightforward to understand, it does have a degree of complexity. In order to get the most out of the software, we needed to invest in staff development. Although basic coding and querying could have been achieved without the training, detailed queries required to achieve the high-level aims of the database would not have been possible without in-depth training. We initially hoped that this could be done in-house, but we eventually had to go to an external training provider. Once the database was established in NVivo, I added additional qualitative data sources to the database and coded them using the same grounded theory technique previously applied. Initially the source attribute for each qualitative data set was captured, including:

- feedback source
- academic year the feedback was received
- actual date the feedback was received.

Demographic attributes of the respondents were coded, linking all comments received to the following characteristics:

- user type (e.g. postgraduate taught, senior lecturer, researcher)
- study mode (full time, part time)
- subject discipline
- campus location
- branch library most commonly used

- fee status
- age range
- gender.

The individual comments were analysed and coded by topic, building on the taxonomy I had previously developed. Initially the topics were very granular in nature with comments coded multiple times. For example, a section of a transcript of an interview with academic staff on their views of library skills training for students could include the following topics:

- information literacy training
- embedded training
- dissertation support
- referencing skills
- student training.

During this process, individual comments were also analysed by their nature: whether positive, negative or making a suggestion. Once I had completed the analysis, the topics were reviewed and grouped, and in some cases merged or separated as the thinking developed.

Using a customer feedback database
This approach to the coding of the qualitative data enabled quick and detailed queries to be run on the feedback in a variety of coding combinations, for example:

- What are the key concerns of the management students?
- What are the top comments received about each branch library?
- Have the part-time students made more positive or negative comments?

We used the data from the customer feedback database to inform key business decisions, such as the procurement of a new cross-searching platform for the libraries. The database was initially interrogated for all information on customer search habits and preferences identified in the research we had previously undertaken. While this provided a good basis for understanding, owing to the scale of the procurement decision we decided we needed to capture more detailed requirements. I conducted a number of focus groups with customers to explore their needs from a cross-searching product. The transcripts of these discussions were added to the database and coded using the same methodology. We analysed both sets of data and combined the findings to create a customer requirements report for the project team.

In addition to answering key business questions to inform decision making, we also used the database annually to create a customer feedback report for all library staff. The feedback report was incorporated into our existing strategic audit processes, where our customers' perceptions and opportunities for improvement were exploited to develop future strategic projects. Verbal presentations of the data were incorporated into the annual all staff away day, allowing a two-way discussion and greater understanding of the issues raised by our customers. I presented the feedback in a holistic manner structured around four main themes:

- *celebrating success*: identifying the strengths of the library service from the perspective of the customer
- *customers' expectations*: highlighting what the customers expect from the library service, and what they do not want the service to provide
- *opportunities for improvement*: issues or areas of the service that are currently not meeting customers' expectations
- *local issues*: specific branch library issues that may require improvement.

These areas inform the identification of issues surrounding the service, which feed into staff discussions on possible options to improve the library service and which are the basis of our annual strategic projects.

Critically, we used the database to advocate the service to senior stakeholders. I combined qualitative data from the customer feedback database with quantitative data received through surveys and other library assessment mechanisms to tell the story of the service, tailored for the audience's needs. Key successes were quickly recognised and incorporated into an annual report to the University's senior management team. The top concerns of customers and the actions planned to overcome them were also reported. Where the actions required were outside the control of the department, for example IT issues, the data was used to influence senior managers into effecting change.

Conclusions, next steps and lessons learned

One of the key lessons learned early on was that the coding for conversations on the library collection was not granular enough. I had coded topics by source type (e.g. journal, e-book, print book), customers' perception (e.g. stock deficiencies, positive comments), and behaviour (browsing, searching). Within a short period, it became apparent that we needed detailed information on customers' perceptions of individual publishers. We sought to expand our collection to alumni and wanted to know which publisher packages to target as a priority. The database did not have the appropriate level of granularity to help identify the publishers. We had to conduct additional primary research to answer the question, but as a result introduced improvements to future coding.

One of the key research questions the database was seeking to answer was 'What are our key customer concerns and how are these changing over time?' The strength of the strategy and the real value will come with ongoing systematic longitudinal analysis, which has yet to be realised.

The customer feedback database has enabled Cranfield Libraries to manage the wealth of qualitative data available, and exploit it quickly and easily. It has enabled us to answer key business questions, increase our understanding of customers' needs, and advocate our service effectively to key stakeholders. Lessons learned from the project include the need to invest in staff training on the qualitative software analysis tool. Coding at a publisher level to enable queries to be run on specific products and providers is also recommended. Overall, we need to ensure that the data available in the library is used to the benefit of the service and its customers.

> ## Case Study 6.2   Digging deeper: using qualitative data analysis of survey feedback to inform library strategy at the University of Oxford
> *Frankie Wilson*

Background

The Bodleian Libraries are a system of 28 libraries that serve the University of Oxford, including the principal University library – the Bodleian Library – which has been a library of legal deposit for over 400 years. Together, they hold more than 13 million printed items, over 80,000 e-journals and outstanding special collections including rare books and manuscripts, classical papyri, maps, music, art and printed ephemera. The University of Oxford is a collegiate research university with a history going back as far as 1096. Today it educates almost 12,000 undergraduates, the same number of graduates, plus more than 14,000 people enrolled on continuing education courses.

In addition to serving the needs of members of the University of Oxford, the Bodleian Libraries are a national research library, and provide services to over 30,000 library card holders who are not members of the University.

The reader survey

The Bodleian Libraries do not have a strong history of undertaking surveys of their whole readership at the same time, but nevertheless took part in the first Society of College, National and University Libraries (https://www.sconul.ac.uk; SCONUL) cohort to undertake LibQUAL+ in 2003. It was not an unqualified success, and so it was not until 2012 that the Libraries ventured to undertake another reader-wide survey. This time the Lite protocol was used, which, despite pushback from some respondents, was better received than the 2003 survey, gathering 3611 responses with 46% leaving comments. The results of the 2012 survey were used to inform Bodleian Libraries' strategic plan 2013–16 and associated imple-mentation plan. As this plan period came to an end, the Libraries decided to re-run a reader-wide survey in order to inform the development of the next strategy.

A reader survey working group was formed, with representatives from all areas of the Libraries. Following investigation of other options, including other standardised surveys and the possibility of an in-house survey, the group decided to use LibQual+ Lite again as it measured not only satisfaction but also expectation levels. Bodleian Libraries was consistently rated one of the top three libraries in the National Student Survey (NSS), which indicated that our student body was very satisfied with our provisions when compared with students' assessments of other university libraries, but we knew we were not fully meeting their expectations and so needed the nuanced 'zone of tolerance' approach (see Chapter 3) that LibQUAL+ offers. We also wanted to compare the priorities of our different reader groups – undergraduates, postgraduates, faculty and external library card holders.

In response to feedback about the 2012 survey, the working group had customised all of the text to reflect British English (e.g. catalogue instead of catalog) and local terminology (e.g. giving the Oxford-specific name of the catalogue). In 2012 we had also had vocal feedback from science and medicine faculty that the survey was not relevant to them, as they did not use any physical library. We therefore presented the demographic questions in a different order on our customised survey – asking about which library respondents used most at the start of the survey, with 'I do not use a physical library' as the default. Unfortunately, we were unable to impose survey logic not to present 'Library as Place' questions to respondents who selected this option. Instead, where respondents had chosen NA (not applicable) for these questions the response did not count when determining exclusion from the aggregate scores.

A further change was made in the timing of the survey – instead of running in term one (summer to Christmas 2015) as in 2012, we ran it in term 2 (Christmas to Easter 2016). This meant that our survey clashed with the NSS, but the University gave us special permission to run it as we were surveying our whole readership, while the NSS only surveyed final year undergraduates.

These changes worked – the response level from students was 13% higher than in 2012, and we received zero complaints about the survey itself!

Surface results
LibQUAL+ has the tag-line '22 items and a box' and this case study focuses on the analysis of the 1,174 free-text comments entered into that box.

The first stage of analysis involved reading every comment to identify those that could be 'quick wins'. The comments were viewed in a spreadsheet, with the answers to the demographic questions included against each comment. Quick win comments complaining about physical aspects of a library were grouped by library and passed on to the relevant librarian in charge; comments complaining about collections were grouped by department and faculty and passed on to the relevant subject librarian; comments complaining about specific aspects of provision (e.g. the website, broken e-resource link in the catalogue) were passed on to the relevant department in the Bodleian Libraries. In addition, specific positive comments (all of which were about staff) were passed on to the staff member and their line manager. Managers in all areas with potential 'quick wins' were required to produce an action plan, and report on their progress against these actions by the end of term 2, so 'you said, we did' could be communicated throughout the University.

Over the next three months I re-read every comment and tagged them for topic and sentiment (positive, negative, neutral). This was an iterative process, as the tagbook developed through this analysis (so as not to impose my preconceived ideas on the data) and when a new tag was added I had to re-read the previous comments to identify those the tag applied to. The most frequent topic commented on was opening hours – all negative. This concurs with the response to the question about opening hours on the survey (one of the local questions), which had a mean average score of 5.8 out of 9.

The other topic where the comments were universally negative was borrowing, or rather the inability to borrow all books. The Bodleian Libraries is a legal deposit library and so is entitled to one free copy of every UK publication; it is charged with preserving the nation's published output for future generations. Therefore, the Bodleian Libraries' policy is that all material so received is for library use only – history shows that the Bodleian Library even refused to lend a legal deposit book to Charles I in 1645 (Clapinson, 2015)! Such books are part of the active collection, with those in demand (e.g. on reading lists) kept on open shelves in a relevant library and all others able to be recalled from the remote store to a reading room. This is a unique situation in a UK university (Cambridge University Library lends its legal deposit books) and the policy is not helpful for students and faculty. We know this because we consistently receive negative feedback on this issue via all our feedback channels.

In the 2012 survey respondents had also commented negatively on the Libraries' opening hours and restricted borrowing rules. While the consequent implementation plan had included projects to improve opening hours, the proposal by the Libraries that legal deposit books might be borrowable produced outrage from faculty (Goodall and Britten, 2012) and therefore was abandoned. With no desire to poke the hornets' nest, the only action available in response to the 2016 results was to try to communicate the reason why these books could not be borrowed.

Digging deeper

In order to 'close the loop' with students who took part, it was considered essential to report the results of the reader survey before the end of term three (June) when taught students would depart for the summer vacation. Unfortunately, by this deadline, the free-text comments had only been analysed at a surface level, as described in the previous section. However, with more time in the summer, and an eye on the strategic planning away day in September where I had been asked to present insights from the reader survey, I continued the analysis through interpretative synthesis.

Despite having access to NVivo, I did not have time to learn how to use it effectively, and so worked with traditional post-it notes (Figure 6.1 on the next page).

I went back to all of the negatively tagged comments and undertook grounded theory coding following Charmaz's approach from her 2006 book. I started with initial line-by-line coding, then focused coding and creating memos, when I brought in contextual

Figure 6.1 *The use of Post-it notes for interpretative synthesis*

information from respondents' demographics. Through iterations I compared data for similarities and differences, and started to relate my categories to each other, proposing underlying theoretic categories. At some point in this process insight struck – dissatisfaction with inability to borrow some books, opening hours, lack of e-books for reading list items were all aspects of a single underlying concept for students: 'lack of access to stuff I need when I want it'. Students do not want to be able to borrow all items for the sake of it; they do not want longer opening hours because they expect university libraries to be open 24/7 or so they can surf the web at 2am; they are not requesting e-books because they are digital natives who prefer to read on screen rather than paper (well, some are). The students most dissatisfied with opening hours were those where most of the materials they needed for their studies were library-use-only items held at a library with short opening hours. Students whose materials were borrowable or online did not mind that the library they used as study space closed at 10pm.

Strategic impact

The insight gained by interpretative synthesis on the LibQUAL+ free-text comments prompted a change in approach to addressing the issues of opening hours and loanable legal deposit books in the new strategic plan. The aim is now to ensure students can access the materials they need at a time determined by them. Extending opening hours, providing borrowable copies, or seeking online versions are ways of achieving this aim – a means to an end, not an end in themselves. This has enabled a nuanced approach, choosing the appropriate option depending on library and subject context, rather than a blanket 'extend library opening hours' approach.

Lessons learned

We will be repeating the reader survey in 2019 and I do not envisage the survey instrument changing from the 2016 version. However, I will be making three significant changes to the analysis of the results based on the lessons learned during the above analysis:

- The data, including the free-text comments, will be put through visualisation software to produce dashboards so librarians-in-charge and subject librarians can read the comments pertinent to them directly to identify 'quick wins'.
- As the reader survey working group will not need to spend time customising the survey, I will ask its members to undertake the tagging (topic and sentiment) of the free-text comments rather than doing this all myself.
- We will use NVivo to facilitate the analysis.

Conclusions

Investing the considerable time necessary to go deeper than tagging the content and sentiment of the feedback comments from the 2016 reader survey has led directly to a change in the Bodleian Libraries' strategy, and so, through the implementation projects, to service improvements. Two well-known subjects of student dissatisfaction – opening hours and library-use-only books – had always been considered impossible to address and improve to students' desired levels. Interpretative synthesis of the data led to insight into the underlying reason for them both, and that what students were asking for was not what they actually wanted. With this knowledge, the new strategic projects have been able to investigate alternative ways of addressing this underlying need, and so to improve student satisfaction.

Case Study 6.3 Let the computer take the strain: automatic analysis of LibQUAL+ free-text comments at Singapore Management University Libraries
Tamera Hanken

Background

Singapore Management University (SMU) Libraries is situated in the heart of SMU's city campus and consists of two libraries, the Li Ka Shing Library (opened in 2005) and the Kwa Geok Choo Law Library (opened in 2017). The SMU Libraries currently serve a community of approximately 9,000 students and 300+ faculty within the schools of business, law, accountancy, economics, information systems and social sciences.

The SMU Libraries' assessment framework is driven by a range of quantitative and qualitative research methods, e.g. analysis of surveys, resource usage data, focus groups, ethnographic and other kinds of user studies. The research is used to make decisions; improve processes, services and user experience; and demonstrate and communicate the value of SMU Libraries to the SMU community.

LibQUAL+

SMU Libraries administered the first LibQUAL+ survey (see Chapter 3 for a description of this methodology) in 2013 and the second in 2015. The third survey will be administered in 2018. In 2015, 2,143 surveys were collected, 86% of whose respondents were undergraduates. The survey provided valuable insight into users' perceptions of service quality in three broad categories: library as place, information control and affect of service.

The 2015 LibQUAL+ survey collected 1,324 free-text comments, primarily from undergraduate students and business students, with library as place the most cited area of comment:

- *Analysed by year of respondent at university*: most comments were made by first-year students (340) and fewest by fourth-year students (236)
- *Analysed by discipline*: most came from the School of Business (505) and fewest from the School of Social Sciences (108)
- *Analysed according to LibQUAL+ categories*: library as place was the most cited category (505 comments, 64% negative).

In large part the comments supported the quantitative LibQUAL+ results.

Design, method, approach

Following the initial manual analysis of the LibQUAL+ comments, there was an interest in exploring further and analysing various aspects of the textual comments. For example, what specifically accounted for the negative comments regarding 'library as place'? The librarians were also interested in finding a more efficient and effective automated method of organising and analysing the comments. Therefore, librarians collaborated with faculty from the School of Information Systems to design and develop an automated solution.

A potential approach was to adapt a survey feedback tool the faculty of the School of Information Systems used to analyse comments of teaching evaluations. The tool would analyse the LibQUAL+ textual comments to discover insights into topics of interest (collections, noise levels etc.) and sentiments (positive or negative) of library users.

Text analytics is a research area that supports mining unstructured data and generates a meaningful representation of the text for decision makers (Aggarwal and Zhai, 2012). In our study, we used the text analytics approach to categorise the comments by topic and extract the sentiments of the comments. Then we transformed outputs into a visual display to help library managers assess and make decisions.

Solution overview

We used a library feedback sentiment analysis tool, which integrated clustering and sentiment extraction algorithms to generate the visual displays for library managers. We first give a general overview of the process and then details of each stage.

The system solution overview consisted of four main stages, as shown in Table 6.2.

Table 6.2 *The four stages of the library feedback sentiment analysis tool used to analyse LibQUAL+ free-text comments at SMU Libraries*

Stage	1	2	3	4
Purpose	Data pre-processing	Topic extraction	Sentiment extraction	Visual summarisation
Tools and techniques	Perl scripts	CLUTO – agglomerative clustering	LingPipe – sentiment classifier	JFreeChart, Apache POI

In stage 1 a matrix of comments is generated after pre-processing the data. In stage 2 comments are clustered according to their primary common topic and then the common top words representing the cluster are extracted. In stage 3 the sentiment of each comment is extracted, and finally in stage 4 topics and sentiments are aggregated for comprehensive reporting. The tool starts with the schools and corresponding comments as inputs, and executes all the stages to generate visual analysis reports.

Data pre-processing

In the data representation stage, first, all terms are extracted from input comments using tokenisation by space – the processor is programmed to recognise that (in English) words are separated by a space character, so uses the presence of a space as a 'cut here' instruction to split a stream of characters into words. Some words such as prepositions and articles are noise and are not useful in the topic and sentiment extraction process, and are removed from each comment using a stop-word list. Each comment is then represented in the form of a table or matrix. Each row denotes a comment, and each cell in that row is occupied by a single word (or feature) from that comment together with its term frequency (log or square root). Such data representation assists in judging the importance of each word in a comment and therefore measuring the similarity between comments. We used Perl scripts to generate the comment-term matrix.

Extracting topics

Clustering is the task of dividing data into distinct groups such that objects in the same clusters are similar and objects in different clusters are dissimilar (Beil, Ester and Xu, 2002).

In our context, comments are considered similar if they contain overlapping words or phrases. Comments on similar topics exhibit specific characteristics that separate them from comments that focus on other topics. For example, comments on the topic 'space' use words such as 'seating', 'noise', 'crowding', etc. We used the tool CLUTO (Karypis, 2015) to generate clusters of comments.

The tool takes a comment-term matrix from the previous stage as input and provides visual displays of the clusters and top words in each cluster as shown in Figures 6.2 and 6.3.

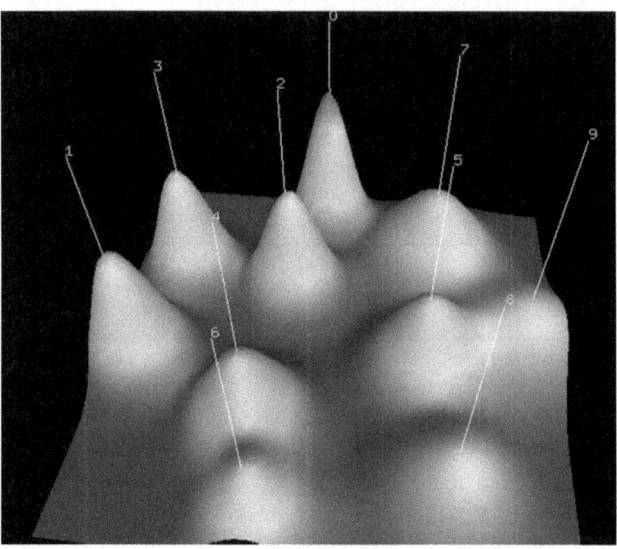

Figure 6.2 *Example of a mountain representation of ten clusters generated by CLUTO*

Quiet	Books	Librarians	Databases
Conducive	Course	Friendly	Search
Noise	Textbooks	Helpful	Resources
Level	Reserves	Help	Online
●	●	●	●

Study			Services
Space	●	●	Pyxis
Spaces			Search
Students			Satisfied

●	●	●	●
Feedback	Services	Hours	Café
Facebook	Excellent	Guys	Hours
People	Provided	People	Air
Survey	Help	Time	Staff

Figure 6.3 *Example of the most frequently used words in several clusters generated by CLUTO*

Figure 6.2 shows the mountain representation of the clusters generated. The colour, shape and height of the peaks represent cluster deviation, distribution of data and cluster similarity, respectively. However, this mountain view is not user friendly for topic and sentiment visualisations. Therefore, in the visual summarisation stage we used visual displays that can demonstrate topics and sentiments in user-friendly charts (Figure 6.3).

Figure 6.3 shows the words used most frequently in comments on several primary topics within each cluster. For example: 'study', 'space', 'spaces', 'students' were used in comments on the topic 'library space'.

Sentiment extraction

Sentiment analysis involves building a system to collect and examine opinions about a topic or product (Hu and Liu, 2004). Sentiment extraction involves labelling the sentiment of a comment as positive or negative. For example, 'Library is always crowded, students are not guaranteed a space to study at times' is a negative comment on space whereas, 'I like the new study space and chairs that are back-friendly' is positive.

During this stage, the objective is to find the overall positive or negative sentiment for a given comment. We used a classification-based approach for this task and created a training set for training the classifier. For this purpose, we used LingPipe Language Identification Classifier (LingPipe; http://alias-i.com/lingpipe), which adopts a sentence-level logical regression classifier. It deconstructs each comment sentence into n-grams, or the number of words evaluated at a time while processing the sentiment of the comment. Bi-grams aid in processing by negating phrases such as 'not good'.

Using bi-grams, LingPipe evaluates two words at a time before assigning an overall sentiment to the comment. This permits evaluation of double negatives allowing for a better evaluation of sentiment. The classifier learns the natural distribution of characters in the language model of a training data set and then assigns a sentiment probability to each evaluated bi-gram according to a probability distribution, eventually leading to an aggregated final sentiment for each comment evaluated.

Visual summarisation

Visual summarisation is the final stage, where the goal is to provide user-friendly summaries of the topics and sentiments obtained from the previous phases. Visualisation charts use the topics, sentiments and schools as inputs. The charts are generated using JFreeChart (Object Refinery Limited, 2015) and inserted into Microsoft Excel files that are generated using Apache POI libraries (Apache Software Foundation, 2002), so they are easy for users to analyse. We adopted the charts similar to feature-based sentiment summaries by Hu and Liu (2004). Figures 6.4 and 6.5 on the next page show sample comments and the visuals of sentiments extracted by our tool.

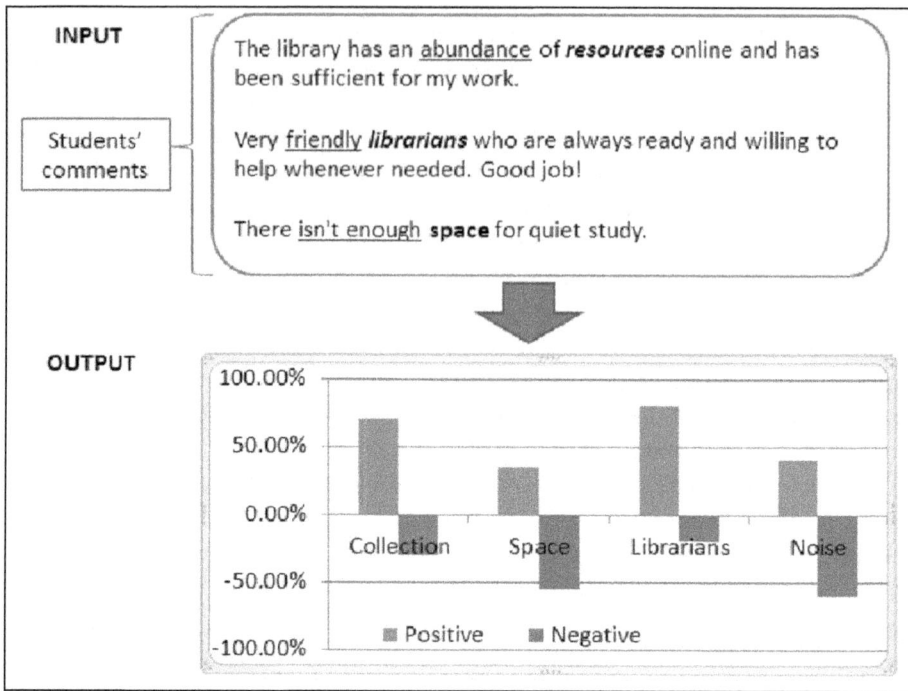

Figure 6.4 *Example comments from library users as input and sentiment classification visual by topic*

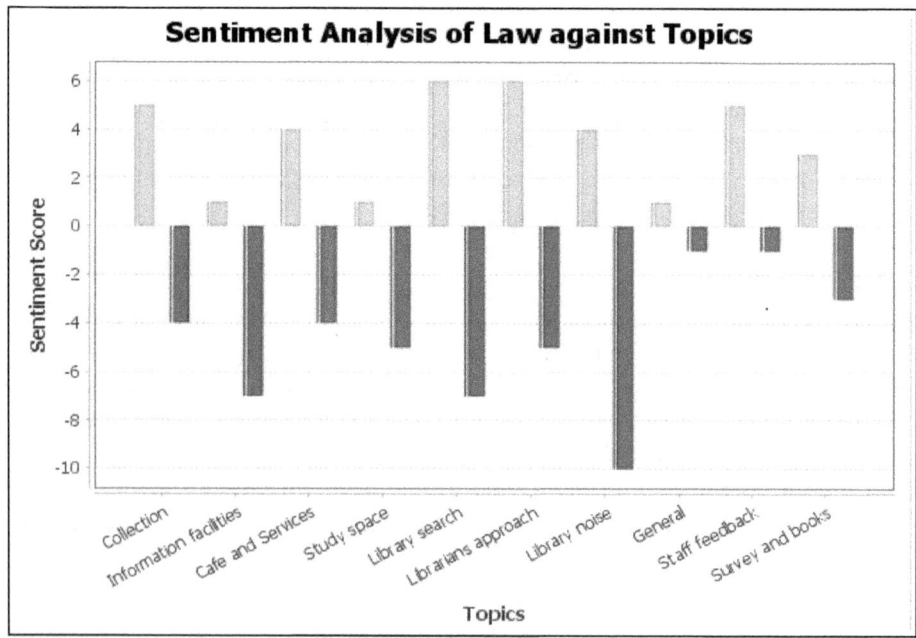

Figure 6.5 *Sentiment analysis of Law School users about the library generated by the library feedback sentiment analysis tool*

Findings

The results from using library feedback sentiment analysis to drill down deeper into student preferences and sentiment about library as place largely reflected the LibQUAL+ survey results. Positive comments about SMU Libraries tended to be very generic, for example: 'The library provides a very conducive place to study', so it was difficult to learn what specifically the students liked, though the most cited specific example was comfortable seating. Fortunately, the students were very specific when stating what they did not like about the Library – what they had strong negative sentiments about, for example: 'Community space/collaborative areas can be contained in a restricted area rather than open places to keep library quiet and conducive for studying', 'More project rooms and increase the table size' and 'The sliding door at the entrance of the Quiet Room at level 2 is forever opening and closing. This distracts users very much and is really noisy.'

Limitations

There are some challenges that we have noticed with using CLUTO for library feedback sentiment analysis. Firstly, the performance of the system in extracting topics and sentiments should be studied in detail and compared with other text analytics techniques. The library feedback sentiment analysis tool offers a sentiment score for each topic being discussed by students but does not go deeper to signify what the actual comments spoke about. Deeper sentiment analysis and the system accuracy are the issues that we need to address in future. Secondly, each comment can only belong to one cluster, so even though a single comment can span multiple topics, it will be clustered under the primary topic – or the topic with most of its discriminating significant words similar to those in the comment, as judged by the clustering function. Topic models such as latent Dirichlet allocation (Blei, Ng and Jordan, 2003) could be helpful to overcome this limitation.

Conclusions

While the library feedback sentiment analysis tool has limitations and the method of text mining and analysis is an area of continued professional development for librarians, the collaboration between SMU Libraries and the School of Information Systems resulted in a number of benefits. The analysis of the LibQUAL+ free-text comments provided insight into what students care most and least about their learning spaces. The comments, especially the negative comments, provide quick win opportunities to make improvements and engage the students in the process, adjusting the sliding doors in the Quiet Area or adjusting the temperature or lighting in other areas of the library. Of more significance, the sentiment and preferences of the Law School students was taken into consideration during the planning of the Kwa Geok Choo Law Library. Likewise, as we plan for reconfiguring the learning and collection spaces at Li Ka Shing Library, the preferences and sentiments of students from the other schools are being analysed and considered.

Conclusions

This chapter has demonstrated that qualitative feedback gathered via surveys and focus groups can be harnessed to improve customers' experience of your library. Exactly the same techniques can be used to get more from unsolicited feedback, such as from feedback forms or social media posts. At the most basic level, simply reading all the responses and identifying the complaints that can be quickly and easily addressed will go a long way to removing the day-to-day irritations of your customers. For such things, a single person reporting it will be the tip of the iceberg.

Although it takes more time than quantitative data analysis, and you may have to explain the paradigm to those to whom you are presenting the findings, undertaking qualitative analysis can lead from mere comprehension to understanding and even insight into your customers' interactions with your library. Therefore qualitative feedback is an assessment goldmine.

Further resources

Bryant, A. and Charmaz, K. (2007) *The Sage Handbook of Grounded Theory*, Sage.
Dey, I. (1993) *Qualitative Data Analysis: a user-friendly guide for social scientists*, Routledge.
Gorman, G. E. and Clayton, P. (2004) *Qualitative Research for Information Professionals: a practical handbook*, 2nd edn, Facet Publishing.
Patton, M. Q. (2014) *Qualitative Research and Evaluation Methods*, 4th edn, Sage.
Silverman, D. (2015) *Interpreting Qualitative Data*, 5th edn, Sage.
Urquhart, C. (2012) *Grounded Theory for Qualitative Research: a practical guide*, Sage

References

Aggarwal, C. C. and Zhai, C. (2012) *Mining Text Data*, Springer Science & Business Media.
Apache Software Foundation (2002) *Apache POI Project*, Apache POI, https://poi.apache.org/.
Beil, F., Ester, M., Xu, X. (2002) *Frequent Term-based Text Clustering*, paper given at the ACM KDD Conference.
Blei, D. M., Ng, A. Y. and Jordan, M. I. (2003) Latent Dirichlet Allocation, *Journal of Machine Learning Research*, **3**, 993–1022.
Charmaz, K. (2006) *Constructing Grounded Theory: a practical guide through qualitative analysis*, Sage.
Charmaz, K. (2013) *Constructing Grounded Theory*, 2nd edn, Sage.

Clapinson, M. (2015) *A Brief History of the Bodleian Library*, Bodleian Library Publishing.

Denzin, N. K. and Lincoln, Y. S. (2005) *The Sage Handbook of Qualitative Research*, Sage.

Dixon-Woods, M., Cavers, D., Agarwal, S., Annandale, E., Arthur, A., Harvey, J., Hsu, R., Katbamna, S., Olsen, R., Smith, L., Riley, R. and Sutton, A. J. (2006) Conducting a Critical Interpretive Synthesis of the Literature on Access to Healthcare by Vulnerable Groups, *BMC Medical Research Methodology*, 6, 35–47.

Glaser, B. G. (1992) *Basics of Grounded Theory Analysis*, Sociology Press.

Goodall, H. and Britten, N. (2012) Bodleian Library Considers Lending Books after 410 Years, *Telegraph*, 13 June, https://www.telegraph.co.uk/education/educationnews/9327429/ Bodleian-Library-considers-lending-books-after-410-years.html.

Hu, M. and Liu, B. (2004) *Mining Opinion Features in Customer Reviews*, paper given at the 19th National Conference on Artificial Intelligence, AAAI'04.

Karypis, G. (2015) Data Clustering Software, *CLUTO: Data Clustering Software*, http://glaros.dtc.umn.edu/gkhome/views/cluto.

Killick, S. (2012) What Do They Want Now? Qualitative regrounding of the LibQUAL+ survey. In Hall, I., Thornton, S. and Town, J. S. (eds), *Proceedings of the 9th Northumbria International Conference on Performance Measurement in Libraries and Information Services,* 197–200, University of York.

Lincoln, Y. S. and Guba, E. G. (1985) *Naturalistic Inquiry*, Sage.

Noblit, G. and Hare, R. (1988) *Meta-Ethnography: synthesising qualitative studies*, Sage.

Object Refinery Limited (2015) JFreeChart, www.jfree.org/jfreechart/.

Orlikowski, W. J. and Baroudi, J. (1991) Studying Information Technology in Organizations: research approaches and assumptions, *Information Systems Research*, 2, 1–28.

Pickard, A. J. (2013) *Research Methods in Information*, 2nd edn, Facet Publishing.

Strauss, A. and Corbin, J. (1998) *Basics of Qualitative Research: techniques and procedures for Developing Grounded Theory*, 2nd edn, Sage.

Wolcott, H. F. (1990) On Seeking and Rejecting: validity in qualitative research. In Preshkin, A. and Eisner, E. W. (eds), *Qualitative Inquiry in Education: the continuing debate*, Teachers College Press, 121–52.

Chapter 7

Emerging techniques

Chapter overview

As our libraries continue to evolve, so too do library assessment techniques. Cutting edge techniques include econometric modelling (Tuomikoski, 2017) and big data (Xu et al., 2017), but in recent years usability testing, ethnographic research, user experience and library analytics have gradually become established in the field of library assessment. This chapter provides an overview of some of the emerging techniques and discusses how they could be applied locally.

The following case studies are presented in this chapter:

- Case Study 7.1 Working with students as partners to understand the needs of distance learners at the Open University (Sam Dick and Keren Stiles, Open University)
- Case Study 7.2 Small-scale user analysis; big library gains at Anglia Ruskin University (Norman Boyd and Hannah Fogg, Anglia Ruskin University)
- Case Study 7.3 Working hard or hardly working? Use of collaborative working space at the University of Bradford (Josie Field, Sarah George and Reshma Khan, University of Bradford).

Case Study 7.1 describes how Dick and Styles work with students to undertake usability testing of the online provision of Open University Library Services. Through setting up a 400–500 member student panel, there is always a group of willing participants ready to test if a proposed change or development improves the student experience. This has enabled the Library to make decisions faster and with more confidence.

As well as demonstrating Anglia Ruskin University Library's commitment to empowering frontline library staff, Case Study 7.2 describes how Boyd and Fogg supported teams of staff to undertake nine projects using five different user experience techniques. This had benefits for their users – directly as a result of changes made in response to the projects' results, and indirectly by giving frontline staff the opportunity to interact with students outside the usual transactions.

In contrast, Field, George and Khan (Case Study 7.3) used multiple forms of observation in a single project. Their unobtrusive observation revealed previously unknown behaviour was taking place in one part of the library under inspection, which led to a more nuanced understanding of how users viewed that area. However, the results gave rise to a crucial question – were students working hard, or hardly working? Applying cyber-ethnographic research techniques alongside the observation showed that they were engaged in productive study sessions.

Usability testing

Apple changed the world of product design when the company produced a device that had no accompanying manual. Users are now used to an environment where they do not have to be trained in using a product because it is obvious how to operate it. Product designers use a methodology called usability testing to evaluate a product's ability to deliver its intended purpose, focusing on ease of use. Usability testing reveals how real users use the system, in contrast with the usability inspection methods employed previously, where experts evaluated a user interface without involving actual users (Barnum, 2002).

Usability testing is commonly used to evaluate websites or applications, computer interfaces, documents and devices. As such, it is applicable to the assessment of library websites, catalogues, self-checkout machines, apps, photocopiers … any situation where users interact with technology. The same principles apply to wayfinding within spaces – users do not want to have to think; they want the next step to be obvious. Therefore, usability testing is also appropriate when investigating library spaces, wayfinding and layouts.

Usability testing involves systematic observation of real users under controlled conditions to determine how well people can use a product for its intended purpose (Nielsen, 1994) and what they do and don't like about it. The first step in this process is to decide who the audience for the website, tool or space is. The next step is to understand what this audience(s) want(s) to do on the website or tool or in the space. With this information it is possible to create scenarios and tasks that accurately represent real world use. Participants have the scenario explained to them, and perform the tasks while investigators observe closely what they do.

Insight into why participants are behaving the way they are is gathered using techniques such as the 'think aloud protocol', where testers describe their thoughts out loud and the observer writes them down; and eye tracking, which uses hardware to determine what the tester is looking at (Blakiston, 2015). The results are used to make changes to the website, tool or space, and the testing is repeated.

This simple, practical user-research method can be undertaken with minimal resources. Nielsen (2000) argues that only five testers are needed per iteration of the design in order to discover most usability problems. Most testing sessions last around 20 minutes, therefore necessitating only a small 'thank you' such as a free coffee voucher, and most front-facing staff have the skills needed to be an observer.

A variation of usability testing is A/B testing. As the name implies, two versions (A and B) are compared, which are identical except for one variation that might influence a user's behaviour. For example, a library website refresh project might test elements such as content text, layout, or use of images and colours, to see what combination makes it easiest for users to find specific elements or information, e.g. the opening hours, compared with the existing site.

User experience: ethnographic research and human-centred design

As we have described in previous chapters, library assessment has evolved from considering only quantitative data into using qualitative research to understand what users think of a library and its services. Research methods such as surveys, focus groups and interviews are widespread. However, such methods rely on self-reporting and therefore do not always elicit accurate information about usage patterns and requirements – humans are notoriously inaccurate at observing what has happened (as demonstrated in the 'invisible gorilla' experiment conducted at Harvard by Simons and Chabris, 1999). Respondents are not able to say what they actually do, or may wish to hide their behaviour if it contravenes library rules. In addition, qualitative research might tell you about what users want the library to provide, but cannot shed light on 'why' (Given, 2006), and therefore provides no insight that can be used when designing the services or spaces to address the documented need.

Ramsden (2016) advocates using ethnographic methods to address this. Ethnography is 'the art or science of describing a group or culture' (Fetterman, 1998, 1) and uses 'a collection of qualitative methods that focus on the close observation of social practices and interactions [to understand] the context in which activities occur' (Asher and Miller, 2011, 3). Library users are a specific group that share ideas, experiences, attitudes and values – a 'culture' – although there are subcultures within library users – students, researchers, teenagers, librarians, etc. Using ethnographic methods to investigate the culture of library users can provide evidence of usage patterns, and insight into how each sub-culture responds to library spaces, policies, services, systems and designs (Ramsden, 2016).

Staff in a number of libraries in the USA have worked with anthropologists using ethnographic methods in assessment for over a decade (Delcore et al., 2009; Duke and Asher, 2011; Foster and Gibbons, 2007; Kim Wu and Lanclos, 2011; McKechnie et al., 2006; Suarez, 2007). However, such work takes time, investment in expertise, commitment to reflection, and acceptance of the risk that what is revealed might contradict long-held beliefs about users' needs and priorities (Lanclos, 2016). It is therefore no surprise that Bryant (2009) stated that ethnography was little used in libraries. However, in 2015 Andy Priestner and Matt Borg changed that with their inaugural international conference 'UX in Libraries' and associated book (Priestner and Borg, 2016) – the *User Experience in Libraries: yearbook 2017* showcases over 20 applications of ethnographic methods in libraries (Priestner, 2017).

Within the broad term 'ethnography' there are numerous methods. The three most commonly applied in libraries are observation, cognitive mapping and interview techniques.

Observation

Ramsden (2016) describes the two dimensions of observation – active and passive (whether the observer participates in the observed activities or not) and covert or overt (whether the subjects know they are being observed or not). She describes the different types of data collection – noting everything observed in as much detail as possible versus creating an *a priori* observation sheet and noting how often each item occurs. This technique was used in projects at the University of Bradford Library (Case Study 7.3).

Cognitive mapping

Cognitive mapping was developed by the Ethnographic Research in Illinois Academic Libraries (ERIAL) Project (Duke and Asher, 2011; Green, Asher and Miller, 2014). They asked participants in a study to create a map of a topic under investigation in six minutes, changing the colour of their pen every two minutes. They observed that participants first drew what was for them the most important or most frequently used aspect of the topic. At the end of the six minutes participants label what they have included and describe and discuss what they have created, including what was omitted. The map can be a geographical map, a plan of a building, a mind map or a drawing of an object.

A number of librarians described using this technique at the UXLibsIII Conference, including Siobhan Morris from the Institute of Historical Research Library (Morris, 2017).

Interview techniques

Design research interview methods get beyond the surface of normal interviewer–interviewee interactions and illuminate feelings and the context of interviewees' behaviour. Three in particular have been used as a starting point for conversations about library usage: the love letter and break-up letter technique; touchstone tours and directed storytelling. Smart Design (2010) developed the love letter and break-up letter technique to try to understand the emotional connection between people and products, services and experiences. Stiles (2017) described using this technique at the UXLibsIII Conference.

In a reversal of the usual 'library tour', a touchstone tour is a guided conversation that uses artefacts in the environment as touchstones for asking questions and acquiring insights (Hanington and Martin, 2012, 89). It can be accomplished by the participant either taking the interviewer on an actual tour, or sending participants to photograph specific 'touchstones', such as 'a place I would never work' or 'something that makes me happy', and then using these photographs as the basis for a conversation. Dodd (2017) described using this method in her presentation at UXLibsIII.

Directed storytelling, developed from the narrative inquiry method used in the social sciences (Clandinin and Connelly, 2000), can illuminate issues and related emotions that might otherwise have been missed or misunderstood by using a more structured interview technique (Hanington and Martin, 2012, 31). The interview begins with the prompt 'Tell me about the last time you used the library'. Additional questions – 'who?', 'what?', 'why?', 'when?', 'how?' – are asked at appropriate points during the narrative. Boyd and Fogg describe using this method in Case Study 7.2.

Lanclos and Asher (2016) sound a note of caution – describing the use of ethnography techniques in libraries as 'ethnographish' as the projects are short term and narrowly contextualised, rather than open-ended and trying to understand the full context of subjects' lives. They do not deny that ethnographish projects have yielded insights and led to positive changes in libraries, but feel they do not lead to a 'different way of seeing'. While not dismissing the advantages that employing a full-time anthropologist to study all aspects of users' behaviour long term can bring, in line with the central ethos of this book, we feel that 'ethnographish' is good enough.

Library analytics

With the move to increasing online provision within education and academic libraries there has been an explosion in big data sets. It is not uncommon for an academic library to have usage data for its electronic resources at an item level for individual customers. As more services are moving online the trend in collection statistics is being replicated in other aspects of library provision. Customer interaction data with online help articles, webchat services, and online information literacy training can be harvested and analysed quickly to identify trends and patterns in library use. Brian Cox from the University of Wollongong provides an easy-to-read 'how to' manual if you want to do this (Cox, 2015).

Early work in moving from usage data analysis to analytics emerged from the University of Huddersfield's Library Impact Data Project (Stone and Ramsden, 2013) where the researchers identified a correlation between library use and student attainment. This early research went on to spawn further studies at eight UK university libraries, all with similar results (Stone et al., 2015). It echoed similar research being conducted in Australia (Cox and Jantti, 2012) and the USA (Soria, Fransen and Nackerud, 2013) at the time. More recently within the wider academic sphere the field of learning analytics has emerged, using big data to understand the characteristics of successful learners with a view to optimising the learning environment (Rienties et al., 2017). As important stakeholders in the learning environment, librarians are considering their role in supporting the learning analytics agenda (Oakleaf et al., 2017). Some librarians are concerned over ethical questions on if and how this information should be used. However, as data analytics becomes an increasing part of the academic institutional infrastructure libraries need to identify the role they will play in this area or risk becoming obsolete and ultimately redundant.

Case Study 7.1 Working with students as partners to understand the needs of distance learners at the Open University
Sam Dick and Keren Stiles

Introduction

The mission of the Open University (OU) is to be 'open to people, places, methods and ideas' and has more students than any other academic institution in the UK. It teaches through a unique method of distance learning, called 'supported open learning'. OU students are motivated by the need to update their skills, get a qualification, boost their career, change direction, prove themselves, or keep mentally active. People of all ages and backgrounds study with us, for all sorts of reasons so there is no such thing as a typical OU student. Over 75% of OU students work full or part time during their studies and more than 17% of our students have a declared disability. The average age of a new undergraduate OU student is now 29 and 30% of our new undergraduates are under 25.

As a result of all our students being distance learners, the OU Library Service focuses on providing students and staff worldwide with access to trusted, quality online library resources and services. A key element of the service is to help students study successfully and increase their digital capabilities. We support teaching and excellence in academic research and scholarship.

Why we involve students

Inspired by the Jisc Summer of Student Innovation (Jisc, 2015) and our need for genuine student insight, we set out to explore ways in which we could work more closely with our distance learners as we developed new tools, systems and services. We weren't in a position to hire students to work alongside us, but by setting up a student panel (described in more detail in the next section) we were able to undertake a wide variety of research including iterative testing of new ideas and prototypes, right through development to launch, and be able to explore wider student experiences, expectations and needs.

Most of our studies of user experience are undertaken remotely online to allow students to participate from any geographic location, so some developments can be tested through unfacilitated projects using first-click testing on wireframes or live websites. Others require facilitated interviews and in those cases we use online meeting or remote support software to facilitate screen sharing. These tools have allowed us to conduct usability testing and other research with user experience techniques such as touchstone tours and love or break-up letters.

By involving students as we develop new tools or service improvements and understanding their needs and experiences more broadly we have greater confidence that we are delivering desirable, accessible, usable and fit-for-purpose tools and services, which meet students' needs and pedagogical requirements. We also have a good idea of what direction a new service or user interface should go in even before we start developing or testing it.

We continue to work towards greater collaboration with students. We would like to involve them more as co-designers and co-creators, as well as user experience research participants. For example in early 2017 we worked with a small group of students to rewrite some of the student-focused pages on our website.

Introducing the student panel

There have been decreasing levels of engagement and responses from students for our bi-annual student surveys for some time, and the last time we ran the survey (2012) the response rate was down to 8%. From 2010 we started usability testing websites and systems, which initially required students to be invited to attend interviews on campus. It was becoming increasingly difficult to get students to engage with any form of research activity regardless of format or method, with the exception of social media. Here we were able to have conversations about a range of products and services that were directly impacting our developments, but it wasn't being used as a formal channel for research projects.

We used this experience of our social media engagement to form the hypothesis that if we could build and develop relationships with students and engage them with the concept of working with us to drive the development of library services (including discussing why they are important) they would be more likely to engage with individual research activities. The student panel (consisting of 400–500 students on a rolling schedule) gives us the mechanism to build these relationships and work more collaboratively.

Our experience in the last four years has shown improvement in two key areas:

● Increased ongoing engagement with members of the panel has drastically improved participation in individual research activities or projects.
● Increased engagement and therefore participation has greatly improved the return on investment of staff time. We are committing slightly more staff time to managing the panel and research and insight projects but are getting a vastly improved quantity and quality of insight and evidence as a result.

What we've learned from our experiences so far

The evidence we gather from the user experience research we conduct with our student panel enables us to make decisions faster and with more confidence. Previously discussions about new developments or alterations to systems or services depended solely on the experiences and opinions of members of library staff, who sometimes had contradictory views or felt out of their depth. Now we can turn to the student panel to ensure that a proposed change or development improves the student experience and use evidence to inform our decision-making process.

Through the mixture of different techniques we are gaining a deeper insight and understanding of what students expect from library services, what they prefer in user interfaces and what sorts of new tools and services we should be turning our attention to. The depth of this understanding enables us to make more robust decisions, and therefore act faster.

We have found that it is very important to mix our research methods and approaches to get a holistic understanding of what students want. We know from previous work that what students say they want or how they perform actions and the actual behaviour they display can often differ. We gain different kinds of insights from interviews and focus groups than from usability testing and other observation methods so our approach has evolved; we now appreciate and use a variety of methods within our research. It is important to plan research and present the findings in a way that gives our colleagues confidence that they are valid and views expressed are representative of a significant proportion of students across all subject areas.

Example 1: Launch and evolution of new discovery interface

We started gathering user requirements for our new discovery interface as we went out to tender for a new library management system. We benchmarked other discovery tools against our own by user testing other libraries' instances of Primo (www.exlibrisgroup.com/products/primo-library-discovery/) and Summon (https://www.proquest.com/products-services/The-Summon-Service.html) and our own EBSCO's Discover Service (EDS; https://www.ebscohost.com/discovery). We also compared these to Google Scholar and Google, knowing that our students are using those anyway. This helped us develop a set of criteria for features, functionality and interface elements that worked well for our students, which we could use to help select our new discovery tool and then help to configure it. As a result the number of complaints we received about the change was low compared with those we had after previous system replacements or redesigns.

Once we had our new discovery tool configured we tested it again before launch in April 2015 to make sure we had met students' requirements. We have continued to test and tweak the interface as new features have become available and when issues have been identified.

Regular website usability testing

Feedback from the students and staff who use our website and the library staff who run our helpdesk has helped us identify user experience issues to investigate. With a collection of online tools such as first-click testing and remote support software we have been able to carry out short user experience studies several times a year to test small improvements to the Library website such as changing terminology, rearranging page content or rearranging a menu in one section.

This way we have been able to avoid our previous cycle of completely redesigning the website every two years, which our students found extremely disruptive. Studying part time as they do, most OU students take six years to complete a degree, so changes every two years led to the perception that the library website was constantly changing and they kept having to 'learn it all over again'. We now work to make sure the website is easy to use and doesn't have to be learned.

Example 2: Student interviews to understand library impact

We have implemented an annual programme of one-to-one student interviews to explore the role the library has played in their studies. This initially stemmed from a desire to be able to find out what impact the library had on students and their study experience beyond resource use data, to understand how they perceive the OU Library and how they would like to see things improve.

There are clear objectives for the interviews but a key part of the approach is that there are very few pre-scripted questions. Staff conducting the interviews are able to follow conversations in an organic way within three broad areas:

- expectations the students had of the library at the start of their studies
- the role of the library during their studies
- what use (or non-use) the students made of the library.

This flexibility allowed interviewers to take the time to explore students' areas of concern and their suggestions, and understand the realities of using library services.

An overview report looks at the key themes for each year as well as themes from previous years. The findings are then grouped and shared with specific service owners for them to action any necessary changes or further investigations. We synthesise each of the interviews into an anonymised one-page case study, which staff can use with colleagues across the University to demonstrate library use or as an advocacy or influencing tool. The findings from the interviews add to our holistic evidence base.

These annual interviews have led us to introduce a number of new developments or changes to services already in place, and provided valuable evidence to influence wider university decisions or initiatives.

Case Study 7.2   Small-scale user analysis; big library gains at Anglia Ruskin University

Introduction

Anglia Ruskin University is a new university situated across four campuses in the east of England. It has 39,400 students from over 185 countries studying for diplomas, and undergraduate and postgraduate degrees. The University Library has 87 staff and provides traditional library services at three of the campuses (Cambridge, Chelmsford, Peterborough), which have 1,460 study spaces and over 260,000 books, over 65,000 e-journals and 230,000 e-books.

Anglia Ruskin University Library's service delivery model was developed from analysis undertaken in 2011 by the University Library's management team. At that point, statistics showed that 70% of all enquiries on the professionally staffed enquiry desk could be handled by library assistants, once they were trained appropriately. Launched in 2012–13, the change freed up professional staff to spend more time in faculty liaison work, and enabled us to streamline our service, creating a single Help Desk within each of the three libraries so we provided one point of contact for our customers. During the same period we made key improvements, which enabled us to deliver a far better range of online support. This included LibGuides from Springshare (https://www.springshare.com) – detailed subject-specific guidance written by subject librarians, used not only by our customers but by the frontline staff too. We moved to Springshare's LibAnswers, providing a robust system to manage online chat, e-mail support and FAQs across a single platform, and the opportunity to record data on queries received at our help desks, around the library spaces, and by telephone. This redesigned service delivery model resulted in an increase in satisfaction as shown by our LibQUAL+ (www.libqual.org) survey, run in April 2014 (and in the most recent 2016 survey too). An additional benefit in this upskilling of staff was an improvement in salary for library assistants (and their concurrent name change to library support advisers) demonstrating recognition of their value in delivering frontline services.

Working with frontline staff

In order to further support the frontline staff we introduced away days (to encourage team-working, bonding, the sharing of experience, etc.), which took place twice a year during quieter times in the academic year (mid-September and mid-January). We used many inventive ways of raising topics for discussion such as reviewing how the new service delivery model had gone, and focusing on a question from staff: 'How far should we go in supporting customers?' As the team matured we also explored the Johnson and Scholes (1988) 'cultural web' model. Practical and consensual actions emerged, leading to line managers being given 'active management' training, the design and creation of a 'core service knowledge quiz' for all library staff, assistant directors undertaking 'back to the floor' sessions to engage with frontline activities, library support advisers swapping jobs across three sites, and a 'free from timetables' day to help frontline staff decide for themselves how to share out duties. We also asked staff to carry out a desk research exercise over the quieter summer period, reviewing the services other academic libraries provided that we might investigate. We decided in January 2016 to demonstrate to our highly skilled staff that we valued their ideas and would like to encourage them to use their skills to understand our customers better and develop ideas for service improvements.

User experience at Anglia Ruskin University Library

Two staff attended the inaugural user experience conference UXLibs (http://uxlib.org/) in Cambridge and set up a user experience group in the University Library. This new method of engaging users was introduced to frontline staff with a view to involving them in investigating library issues. After engaging Andy Priestner to run training at our two larger sites in January 2016, we outlined what we wanted staff to do, and deliberated over how much control we should exert. Over a four month period after the training, staff were given an hour away from frontline duties to plan a project, and then in late May (after the major undergraduate assessment period) they were scheduled to gather their findings and create a presentation for their peers. We ran in-house learning sessions in ideation (idea generation) in order to inspire lateral thinking on the chosen topics. We knew this was not pure ethnographical research or even user experience but it mirrored what Lanclos and Asher (2016) describes as 'ethnographish'.

Would we need to steer groups away from duplicating techniques? Would issues perceived by frontline staff be incompatible with resource provision or existing estate? These proved to be legitimate but unfounded concerns as only two groups on one of our sites chose to use graffiti walls (https://prezi.com/xdyqwmdbnxyv/peterborough-ux-project/), and when it was explained there are many other ways to tackle an issue, one group changed their technique. We gave each group ownership of their project in order to help them develop as a team; we allowed a variety of types of people to engage and encouraged them to value each other's opinions. We also decided to allow failure. None of the projects followed a single methodology outside our framework for providing feedback. We aimed for the projects to be run in the early part of the second semester (from February onwards).

Projects
Love or break-up letters
One group focused on asking customers to write a love letter or break-up letter to a service or part of the University Library, in an abridged version of the user experience technique. The group set up a standalone display with examples on a display board and provided blank index cards. They tried to encourage responses by linking it to Valentine's Day. This gave us several interesting points of feedback, for example one student commented on our automated doors: 'Thank you for never working and always making me look like a girl that doesn't know a thing.' We found this visual technique was popular with staff; one person suggested we should record students reading their letter aloud.

Graffiti boards
The teams using a graffiti board decided to suggest a theme to customers, varying by campus:

- 'If you have a question in the Library how do you ask for help?' and 'What other ways of asking for help would you like us to offer?' (Cambridge)
- 'In the Library, what makes you feel [happy, confused, angry]?' with accompanying emoticons (Chelmsford)
- In the first week 'What do you think of our opening hours?' and in the second 'What do you think of noise levels?' (Peterborough).

Staff at the larger sites found it interesting to note that the positioning of the boards led to different numbers of responses. They were conflicted about whether to respond to suggestions on the board, this being a new very public communication form, and saw that students were not so worried and answered each other's queries. Staff were surprised when customers suggested we introduce services we have offered for some time, such as online chat.

Behavioural mapping

Two projects that had immediate gains for customers followed from observing customers' movements around and in the journal shelving, and how they handled the self-service machines. For the first, a map was created based on the observations; staff concluded that few people used the physical journals during the allocated observation times. As a by-product of the exercise the map demonstrated how far users had to walk around the shelving to collect work from printers. As a result of their observations, the group measured an alternative space and organised for the journals to be moved to a quieter location. A similar project investigated whether moving the rack containing newspapers would increase usage. They tidied the rack and then observed whether customers started to use the newspapers more than in the past: the conclusion was reached easily.

In the second project the group observing the self-service machines noted how frequently each of the three machines were used (62% of users scanned their ID cards successfully) and made recommendations about screen wording, for example simply adding the word 'all' in this sentence: 'Place items to be returned in the opening below.' In feeding back the group stated, 'It was hard to remain as an observer during busier periods'.

Touchstone tours

A team in Chelmsford observed how students used newly installed multifunction devices, which incorporate printing, scanning and photocopying functions, and carried out short interviews with users. Questions asked were whether it was the customer's first time using the new hardware and about their experience. They also asked how users found out about the functions (results were: 38% from our frontline staff, 24% from another user and 16% from our marketing). Interviewees were asked to map their feelings to an emoji chart asking happy (84%), confused (14%), upset (3%) or angry (none).

In Cambridge, under the theme 'Take *us* on a tour of your Library' a group of three staff individually engaged customers as they entered the library and asked if they could follow them as they moved around the library, asking them a few clarification questions as they used services and systems.

After the sessions one member of staff observed, 'This is not surveying by another means, but allowing the customer to talk.' They created a cribsheet of prompts and made notes, but found they needed to engage more directly with users, not just make notes, therefore listening skills and memory are essential tools. In their presentation to their peers, this group summed up the tours as '4 hours, 21 tours = 213 "bits" of data', referring to the variety of ways each staff member coded their data. This led to questions, for example about how to decide whether a statement is positive, negative or both, and for whom, the user or the library, e.g. 'The Help Desk people are lovely [positive], although people can be short with users sometimes [negative], empathises that they must get many repetitive questions [?]'.

The team made interesting observations about the process: 'People tend to use the library to "top up" their study experience', 'Users happy to give time to help us when approached', 'For every assumption, there is a counter-assumption, e.g. tolerance of noise, wanting "background noise"' and 'UX method as beneficial for us as for our users – great to just talk to students and tease out detail'.

Conclusions

These user experience projects worked very well for staff and customers. Frontline staff engaged in a different way from usual and had their assumptions challenged. The staff who delivered the projects presented the conclusions and recommendations. Most focused on issues that, although not completely in keeping with user experience methods, allowed them to tackle a perceived problem in a different way, enabling them to take ownership (with minimal input from more senior staff). Many staff acknowledged that their projects could have been more productive and conclusive if run for longer periods or at different times and days, which will be taken on board for this year's round of user experience activities. One major by-product from the projects was that we learned once more how talented our staff are in presenting findings and making recommendations.

Case Study 7.3 Working hard or hardly working? Use of collaborative working space at the University of Bradford
Josie Field, Sarah George and Reshma Khan

Introduction

The University of Bradford was established in 1966, and is known for pioneering the development of new course subjects to reflect and anticipate the needs of employers. The 1,650 staff work with over 9800 students, 21% of whom are from outside the UK. The J. B. Priestley Library was built in 1975 as the main library serving the University of Bradford. The upper three floors (floors 0–2) underwent extensive refurbishment in 2010–12, when the roof was remodelled with light wells and large windows replaced the original 'arrow-slits' facing the green space known as the amphitheatre.

This refurbishment vastly improved the ambience of the floors by enhancing natural light and airflow. However, the removal of internal walls and soft surfaces to improve the airflow decreased the soundproofing of the floors, leading to concerns about noise transmission between floor 2 (the silent floor) and floor 1 (a large open space originally designated as 'quiet' but now more realistically badged as a space for 'collaborative working'). Library staff's perception was that floor 1 was noisy and not used productively, but beyond vague survey comments about noise there was little evidence to substantiate this. With this in mind, an ethnographic research project was undertaken to investigate the use of the floor 1 study space. The study used various modes of observation, aiming to get a clearer picture of how students used the space.

Methodology

We used an ethnographic approach in examining space usage intending to avoid common pitfalls of traditional social research methods based on self-reporting. Although ethnographic research methods provide rich sets of interesting data on users' opinions, when self-reporting of space assessment they can be more complex. As Jerolmack and Khan's study (2014) notes, it can be problematic to infer behaviour from verbal accounts. Ethnography eliminates the possibility that a user's self-perceptions can diminish research reliability. Instead, the most prominent limitation of ethnography is 'observer influence'.

As users frequently mistook the graduate trainee in the J. B. Priestley Library for a student, it was decided to use this as a unique advantage. The team member observed the space as non-disruptively as possible from a covert observation post, a very specific type of ethnographic research. The graduate trainee sat on floor 1 with a laptop and notepad next to several others with the same equipment, and non-intrusively observed the behaviour within the space. In using this approach we attempted to disrupt traditional power dynamics between 'researcher' and 'researched' and 'librarian' and 'student' and hoped to create a more in-depth understanding of how students really used the space. It is also noteworthy that this research approach avoided contributing to 'survey fatigue' where students are frequently surveyed and become disengaged in efforts to gather information on them. Other than signs on the doors of the zone, there were no obvious 'research interactions' taking place.

This mode of undertaking covert ethnography was paired with student learning champions (students working part time in the library) and library staff carrying out more overt observations, working to balance any observer bias and influence that could have been at play.

In Sheffield Hallam University's study of behaviour in learning spaces staff noted the difficulty in identifying where activities they recorded took place from their observation notes (Turpin et al., 2016). This issue was overcome in the Bradford study by observing a single smaller space and using a coded floorplan where corners of the room were identified by letters, for example 'BL' meant bottom left corner – corresponding to an area labelled BL on the shared floorplan. This eliminated confusion when various observers described activities taking place on floor 1.

This method was very low cost, involving little staff time (a couple of days) and few resources for the amount of rich data it gathered. The only essential resource is a researcher who fits the demographic they are observing; in an academic library this is someone who seems like a student (who come in all shapes and sizes). In this case the observer fitted well with the perceived average age of people using floor 1. Aside from this necessity, the research relies heavily on pre-existing data; the general day-to-day happenings in the library.

However, like any research method this covert ethnographic research approach had disadvantages. In avoiding self-reporting bias there was instead potential for observer bias or misinterpretation of events. It was noted that sometimes the researcher could not decide from students' behaviour whether they were engaging in work or a leisure activity. For example if they were watching videos they could be students studying film or students watching a film for leisure, or those using a laptop could be doing anything from writing a thesis to browsing social media.

In addition to using a variety of observers and a primary researcher with few preconceptions of the space, to combat any potential bias the observations were reported in 'snapshot' moments rather than trying to piece together narratives, avoiding the assumptions that often come in bridging gaps in knowledge in order to 'tell a story'.

Another way we combatted observer bias was by adopting another innovative form of ethnography: cyber-ethnography. It became apparent from conversations with student learning champions that a large part of the culture on floor 1 revolved around the now defunct social media app YikYak, so the researcher created an anonymous YikYak account to view statuses posted in the vicinity of floor 1.

Surprisingly cyber-ethnography seems a yet largely unexplored research method in libraries but one that could prove invaluable given students' typically heavy use of social media (Lau, 2017). This allowed students to air their views on the space anonymously, without being aware of observation, and the insight of a student given via social media provided another important angle to the study. It was also very useful in allowing a member of staff to gather the opinions of students where both parties remain anonymous and the user was not under any pressure to reply in a self-reporting, survey-style manner or with any fear of consequences. This added another dimension to the overall research approach. Through reacting to the different modes of observation available pragmatically, staff employed both a covert and passive approach and a more covert and active approach during the observation period.

Findings

The comments made on YikYak ranged dramatically. One user complained about the social side of the space in worryingly gendered terms, highlighting the potential negative implications of social study spaces becoming too 'social': 'Getting judged by other girls is literally the only reason I hate coming into the library. It's like they're not there to study but to hawk each other out.'

Other comments attempted to 'self-police' the library as a study space with limited noise, demonstrating the responsibility students often took when given an environment with a level of autonomy over their behaviour, such as floor 1 being a designated 'collaborative working' zone: 'To all those people that think sitting outside fl2 doors + shouting on the phone because the walls are sound proof . . . they're really not.'

On one noisy afternoon the graduate trainee ceased to be an entirely passive observer and became more active in engaging in the social media life of the space. At around 3pm on one of the observation days, the researcher posted on YikYak anonymously, asking: 'How can anyone even work on floor 1?!' Someone replied that these were in fact 'ideal conditions' for working. The researcher noted that this seemed contrary to the behaviour being observed, as one of their recurrent observations was that 'people seem well intentioned to work but descend into chatting v. easily'.

The findings from the cyber-ethnography re-enforced the wider results of the observational research – despite staff's perceptions, most students using floor 1 seemed to set out with an intention to work. The observations pointed to the space being used as overflow from the lack of group study rooms created by the refurbishment. Groups, pairs and individuals all used the area for work and discussion and most people brought with them equipment needed to study (laptops, notebooks, etc.). It seemed that users did not mind the noise level. Some people working alone used headphones where sound leakage occurred, which would not have been welcome in a silent study space, and most people spoke at some stage. The only disruptive element of floor 1 was the gathering of larger groups of ten or more students and even this was not a constant issue as most groups were counted as between three to six students, a predictable size of a group working on a project or presentation.

The researcher noted that the signage on floor 1 was inconsistent, commenting that floor 1 'would benefit from better space definition' as the same floor had signs saying 'Quiet Work', 'Work Zone' and 'Collaborative Work', which created an inconsistent message. It was posited that this contributed to staff's perceptions of the area as being a problem zone as there was no consistent idea of how it would ideally function. It seemed that students understood the floor to be a collaborative working area, whereas staff saw it as a failed 'quiet zone' – neither were right or wrong given the signs displayed.

Conclusions

This revelation leads to some final considerations on the research project and its methodology. Ethnographic observation used as a single method can be revealing in observing the unaltered behaviour of students in a space, but it leaves a crucial element out of the picture without being supplemented by research directly interacting with the users. Pairing this kind of observational research with a student survey or even more extensive cyber-ethnographic research would provide the opportunity to explore potential disparities between actual and perceived behaviour from a student's perspective more thoroughly and, importantly, investigate their opinions on what is ultimately their work space.

This additional approach could potentially bridge staff's perceptions, observed behaviour and students' perceptions to create a triangulated understanding of the study space. However, it is worth noting that even as a single method, the observation produced ideas contrary to some staff's opinions and began to create a multidimensional idea of floor 1. It became apparent that although staff felt as though they witnessed all behaviour in the space, often they did not. Since they worked as staff members on floor 1, they inevitably did not actually observe the full range of usage occurring.

Following this research, there has been a reinvigorated library-wide reconsideration of zoning and physical design of space informed by the actual use of space witnessed during the observation period. The signage on floor 1 has been altered and it is now consistently described as a 'collaborative working zone' – a key recommendation from the research.

Conclusions

This chapter has described three of the emerging techniques in library assessment. Use of the first two, usability testing and user experience evaluation, has developed beyond their innovative early users and they are now being adopted more widely. They both emphasise the importance of not assuming anything – from what your customers want from your website to how easy it is to find the photocopier, from why students study where they do to how the décor makes them feel. Usability testing and user experience evaluation both have a collaborative approach to working with customers, rather than the classic researcher–participant dynamic.

There are not many examples of the third approach – library analytics – being used (possibly due to the lack of an engaging annual conference such as UXLibs), but the future importance of relating library usage data to the aims of the parent organisation cannot be underestimated.

Further resources

Anthropologizing: http://anthropologizing.com/about/

Blakiston, R. (2015) *Usability Testing: a practical guide for librarians*, Rowman & Littlefield.

Bryman, A. (2016) *Social Research Methods*, Oxford University Press.

Cox, B. (2015) *How Libraries Should Manage Data: practical guidance on how, with minimum resources, to get the best from your data*, Chandos.

Hanington, B. and Martin, B. (2012) *Universal Methods of Design: 100 ways to research complex problems, develop innovative ideas, and design effective solutions*, Rockport Publishers.

Krug, S. (2014) *Don't make me think revisited! A common sense approach to web and mobile usability*, 3rd edn, New Riders.

Priestner, A. (ed.) *User Experience in Libraries Yearbook*, UX in Libraries.

Priestner, A. and Borg, M. (eds) (2016) *User Experience in Libraries: applying ethnography and human-centred design*, Routledge.

UKLibs: http://uxlib.org/

References

Asher, A. D. and Miller, S. (2011) *So You Want to Do Anthropology In Your Library? Or,*

a practical guide to ethnographic research in academic libraries,
www.erialproject.org/publications/toolkit.

Barnum, C. M. (2002) *Usability Testing and Research*, Longman.

Blakiston, R. (2015) *Usability Testing: a practical guide for librarians*, Rowman & Littlefield.

Bryant, J. (2009) What Are Students Doing In Our Library? Ethnography as a method of exploring library user behaviour, *Library and Information research*, **33**, 3–9.

Clandinin, D. J. and Connelly, F. M. (2000) *Narrative Inquiry: experience and story in qualitative research*, Jossey-Bass.

Cox, B. (2015) *How Libraries Should Manage Data: practical guidance on how, with minimum resources, to get the best from your data*, Chandos Publishing.

Cox, B. L. and Jantti, M. (2012) Capturing Business Intelligence Required for Targeted Marketing, demonstrating value, and driving process improvement, *Library and Information Science Research*, **34**, 308–16.

Delcore, H., Mullooly, J., Scroggins, M., Arnold, K., Franco, E., and Gaspar, J. (2009) *The Library Study as Fresno State*,
http://fresnostate.edu/socialsciences/anthropology/documents/ipa/
TheLibraryStudy(DelcoreMulloolyScroggins).pdf

Dodd, L. (2017) User eXperience . . . our experience at Maynooth University Library. In Priestner, A. (ed.), *User Experience in Libraries Yearbook*, UX in Libraries, 116–20.

Duke, L. M. and Asher, A. D. (eds) (2011) *College Libraries and Student Culture: what we now know*, American Library Association.

Fetterman, D. M. (1998) *Ethnography: step-by-step*, Sage.

Foster, N. F. and Gibbons, S., (eds) (2007) *Studying Students: the undergraduate research project at the University of Rochester*, Association of College and Research Libraries.
https://urresearch.rochester.edu/institutionalPublicationPublicView.action
?institutionalItemId=7044&versionNumber=1

Given, L. (2006) Qualitative Research in Evidence-based Practice: a valuable partnership, *Library Hi Tech*, **24**, 376–86

Green, D., Asher, A. D. and Miller, S. (2014) *ERIAL Project*, www.erialproject.org.

Hanington, B. and Martin, B. (2012) *Universal Methods of Design: 100 ways to research complex problems, develop innovative ideas, and design effective solutions*, Rockport Publishers.

Jamieson, H. (2016) Spaces for learning? Using ethnographic techniques. In Priestman, A. and Borg, M. (eds), *User Experience in Libraries: applying ethnography and human-centred design*, Routledge, 173.

Jerolmack, C. and Khan, S. (2014) Talk Is Cheap: ethnography and the attitudinal fallacy, *Sociological Methods & Research*, **43**, 178–209.

Jisc (2015) *Summer of Student Innovation 2014*, Jisc,
    www.jisc.ac.uk/rd/projects/summer-of-student-innovation-2014.
Johnson, G. and Scholes, K. (1988) *Exploring Corporate Strategy*, 2nd edn, Prentice
    Hall.
Kim Wu, S. and Lanclos, D. (2011) Re-imagining the Users' Experience: an
    ethnographic approach to web usability and space design, *Reference Services
    Review*, **39**, 369–89.
Lanclos, D. (2016) Embracing an Ethnographic Agenda: context, collaboration and
    complexity. In Priestman, A. and Borg, M. (eds), *User Experience in Libraries:
    applying ethnography and human-centred design*, Routledge.
Lanclos, D. and Asher, A. D. (2016) Ethnographish: the state of the ethnography in
    libraries, *Weave: Journal of Library User Experience*, **1**.
Lau, W. W. F. (2017) Effects of Social Media Usage and Social Media Multitasking on
    the Academic Performance of University Students, *Computers in Human Behavior*,
    68, 286–91.
McKechnie, L. E. F., Dixon, C. M., Fear, J. and Pollak, A. (2006) Rules of
    (mis)conduct: user behavior in public libraries, *Proceedings of the Annual
    Conference of CAIS/Actes du Congres annuel de l'ACSI* http://www.cais-
    acsi.ca/ojs/index.php/cais/article/viewFile/580/216.
Morris, S. (2017) Impact in the Institute: conducting UX research in the Institute of
    Historical Research Library. In Priestner, A., *User Experience in Libraries: yearbook
    2017*, UX in Libraries.
Nielsen, J. (1994) *Usability Engineering*, Morgan Kaufmann.
Nielsen, J. (2000) *Why You Only Need to Test with 5 Users*, Nielsen Norman Group,
    https://www.nngroup.com/articles/why-you-only-need-to-test-with-5-users/.
Oakleaf, M., Whyte, A., Lynema, E. and Brown, M. (2017) Academic Libraries and
    Institutional Learning Analytics: one path to integration, *Journal of Academic
    Librarianship*, **43**, 454–61.
Priestner, A. (2017) User *Experience in Libraries: yearbook 2017*, UX in Libraries.
Priestner, A. and Borg, M. (eds) (2016) *User Experience in Libraries: applying
    ethnography and human-centred design*, Routledge.
Ramsden, B. (2016) Using ethnographic methods to study library use. In Priestner, A.
    and Borg, M. (eds), *User Experience in Libraries: applying ethnography and human-
    centred design*, Routledge, 9–20.
Rienties, B., Nguyen, Q., Holmes, W. and Reedy, K. (2017) A Review of Ten Years of
    Implementation and Research in Aligning Learning Design with Learning
    Analytics at the Open University UK, *Interaction Design and Architecture(s)
    Journal*, **3**, 134–54.

Simons, D. J. and Chabris, C. F. (1999) Gorillas in Our Midst: sustained inattentional blindness for dynamic events, *Perception*, **28**, 1059–74.

Smart Design (2010) *Breakup Letter Creative Meeting*. Paper presented at IIT Design Research Conference 2010, 28 June, http://vimeo.com/11854531.

Soria, M. K., Fransen, J. and Nackerud, S. (2013) Library Use and Undergraduate Student Outcomes: new evidence for students' retention and academic success, *Portal: Libraries and the Academy*, **13**, 147–64.

Stiles, K. (2017) UX Research with Distance Learners.In Priestner, A. (ed.), *User Experience in Libraries Yearbook*, UX in Libraries, 127–31.

Stone, G. and Ramsden, B. (2013) Library Impact Data Project: looking for the link between library usage and student attainment, *College and Research Libraries*, **74**, 546–59.

Stone, G., Sharman, A., Dunn, P. and Woods, L. (2015) Increasing the Impact: building on the library impact data project, *Journal of Academic Librarianship*, **41**, 517–20.

Suarez, D. (2007) What Students Do When They Study in the Library: using ethnographic methods to observe student behavior, *Electronic Journal of Academic and Special Librarianship*, **8**, 1–19.

Tuomikoski, K. (2017) Does the gravity Model Hold at Micro-distances? Investigation into University of Oxford students' library choices, *12th International Conference on Performance Measurement in Libraries*, 130–43.

Turpin, B., Harrop, D., Oyston, E., Teasdale, M., Jenkin, D. and McNamara, J. (2016) What Makes an Informal Learning Space?. In Priestner, A. and Borg, M. (eds), *User Experience in Libraries: applying ethnography and human-centred design*, Routledge, 155–72.

Xu, S., Du, W., Wang, C. and Liu, D. (2017) The Library Big Data Research: status and directions, *International Journal of Software Innovation*, **5**, 77–88.

Chapter 8

More than measuring: using assessment holistically

Chapter overview

In this final substantive chapter we turn our attention to ways of using the results of assessment activities, in particular the power of taking a holistic approach to library assessment.

As described in Chapter 1, what makes library assessment different from performance measures and indicators is that the information gathered and/or results of analysis are used to drive change or communicate with stakeholders. The assessment activities presented in previous chapters are powerful forces for service improvement in their own right, but bringing the outputs together enables library staff to acquire a deeper understanding of users' needs and the impact of service changes, and to tell the story of the library service or customer experience as a whole.

In this chapter we discuss how the method of presenting the results of assessment activities is as important as the results themselves. We present case studies where data sets have been successfully combined to generate deeper understanding, and where the results of assessment activities have been used to advocate successfully on behalf of the library service.

The following case studies are presented in this chapter:

- Case Study 8.1 Departmental reporting at the University of York (Vanya Gallimore, University of York)
- Case Study 8.2 University Library Services Sunderland: articulating value and impact through visual presentation of combined data sets (Kay Grieves, University Library Services Sunderland).

Both the University of York and University of Sunderland library services took as their starting point the needs of a particular target group. Both planned data collection to evidence whether the library service was successful in meeting these needs – in Sunderland's case designing new, appropriate collection methods, whereas York identified existing sources of data and feedback. Through focusing on a holistic approach, using all appropriate sources of information, staff in each of the library services gained insights into how to improve the support they offer to the specific group. They were then able to demonstrate the impact of making such improvements, so completing the iterative plan–do–check–adjust cycle of continuous improvement (Deming, 2000).

The University of York Library Service produces a highly visual presentation of a report covering three areas: a summary of the past year, the impact of the previous year's actions, and proposed actions for the coming year. The report is written in a highly narrative style, to explain and contextualise the data, which is essential as the PDF will be circulated more widely than those able to attend the presentation of the report by the librarian who wrote it. Library staff at the University of Sunderland also distribute their message widely – via an online infographic. They therefore use qualitative feedback, including incorporating dynamic media such as videos to provide the context for quantitative data.

The University of Sunderland case study shows that there is no need for a different approach when advocating for a whole service. Staff applied the same model as they used for a specific group: starting with the strategic priorities of their audience; thinking about their desired outcomes, value and impact; explaining how the library services contribute to these expected outcomes; collecting evidence for this contribution; and finally collating and reporting on this evidence holistically. The innovative use of a single page graphical presentation ensures that readers can see the direct link between objective, service offer, engagement, value and impact.

A holistic approach

As Donne's famous poem 'Devotions' declares 'No man is an island entire of itself', similarly libraries do not operate in isolation. Historically, unless very small, libraries have been organised in silos, structured either around functional operations – acquisition, circulation, information skills teaching, etc. – or population groups. However, viewing the outputs of assessment activities in the same way risks not only seeing a single piece of the jigsaw puzzle in isolation, but also missing the opportunity to acquire deeper understanding of the needs of library users as a whole, and different options of how these needs could be addressed.

Furthermore, as Cox and Jantti write, 'Libraries need compelling evidence that directly links their activities to positive outcomes' (2012, 309), and evidence that only illuminates one part of the whole cannot be compelling, because there are too many options for arguing that the demonstrated positive outcome is due to something else.

Social scientists have advocated a mixed methods approach for decades as a way of addressing the inadequacies of quantitative and qualitative methods (Creswell and Plano Clark, 2011). However, taking a holistic approach to assessment is not about ensuring that both the qualitative and quantitative boxes are ticked. Instead, it is concerned with bringing together all the ways of measuring a particular aspect of library provision or service. For example, assessment of an interlibrary loan service involves not only reviewing the usage statistics and satisfaction with the service by users, but also awareness of the service by non-users, provision of resources as part of the main collections (print and online), availability of free online versions (whether legal or not), appetite for waiting for an item, and so on.

Assessment for advocacy

Advocacy is 'the act . . . of pleading for, support for, or recommendation of a person or thing' (Oxford English Dictionary, 2011). In libraries, it typically means arguing for funding. Libraries have long ceased to be able to rely on the argument that they are *a good thing* and therefore should be appropriately funded (e.g. Kean, 2016). Instead, libraries must make an evidence-based case to stakeholders in order to convince them that providing the library with appropriate funding will help stakeholders achieve their goals.

Lanclos describes this as 'constructing a compelling narrative' (2015, 108), arguing that libraries need to engage in 'grounded storytelling' in order to draw attention to their value. Lanclos' argument is predicated on her anthropology background – since first developing language humans have told stories to other humans (Smith et al., 2017). In contrast to this deeply rooted human activity, pie charts are an extremely recent method of communication.

To construct a compelling narrative, the first, crucial, step is to determine what the audience is interested in. Advocacy needs to be specifically tailored for each group of stakeholders, otherwise it will not be compelling to them. There can be no 'one size fits all' approach. However, this does not mean that all aspects of the advocacy must be unique – the same assessment outputs can be re-used for different stakeholder groups, but the specific message must be tailored for the audience.

Once clear what the audience is interested in, the second step is to make explicit how the library contributes to that area of interest. It is extremely unlikely that the library will be the only contributing factor, but instead will be one of a number of necessary contributors, possibly interlinked, possibly discrete. Articulating this contribution can be difficult; it may help to think of the negative situation – what would not occur if the library (or specific library service) ceased to exist.

The final step is to convey the compelling, evidence-based argument in a way that the audience instinctively understands. Modern data visualisation tools can be of great assistance in this (Few, 2013), embodying the idiom 'a picture is worth a thousand words'. Visualisations range from familiar charts and graphs (e.g. pie charts), to innovative ways of presenting similar data (e.g. tree diagrams) and infographics.

Case Study 8.1 Departmental reporting at the University of York
Vanya Gallimore

Introduction

The University of York was founded in 1963 on the principles of excellence, equality and opportunity for all. It now educates nearly 16,000 students in more than 30 departments, with most located on the attractive Heslington campus and the remainder in York city centre's historic King's Manor. As a dynamic, research-intensive university, York is a proud member of the Russell Group of elite universities and committed to developing life-saving discoveries and new technologies to tackle some of the most pressing global challenges.

The University of York Library is made up of seven buildings, including the Borthwick Institute for Archives, providing over 1,250 study spaces. The collections include almost a million printed books and over 18,000 e-journals, and special collections of rare books, manuscripts and archives.

The University of York Library has routinely collected survey and statistical data in order to assess the value and impact of library services over time. In 2014, the Library's Relationship Management Team was restructured into functional areas (academic liaison, research support and teaching and learning). This provided an excellent opportunity to do something tangible and meaningful with the survey and statistical data collected, and to use it to transform how the Library understands, engages with and supports academic departments. The result was the introduction of annual action plans for each academic department, which are written by academic liaison librarians in partnership with their departmental academic colleagues. Action plans are now central to the work of the Relationship Management Team at York and have helped to redefine and strengthen the Library's relationships across the University.

The purpose of the action plans

The primary role of academic liaison librarians at the University of York Library is to build strong, meaningful relationships with academic departments, so library staff can identify departmental needs and ensure they are reflected in service developments for academic staff and students. Academic liaison librarians work closely with academic departments throughout the year, responding to enquiries, attending departmental meetings, delivering digital skills sessions and ensuring that the Library's online and print collections support departmental research and teaching needs. The annual action plans bring together the academic liaison librarians' departmental knowledge with a variety of library assessment data, including the National Student Survey (NSS; https://www.thestudentsurvey.com) and surveys from LibQUAL+ (www.libqual.org), to create a dynamic and holistic framework for ongoing library support of individual departments.

In particular, each action plan aims to:

- provide an annual opportunity for the library and each academic department to work in partnership alongside other year-long relationship-building activities
- demonstrate the impact and value of the library for departments through a range of qualitative and quantitative measures including investment and usage data
- summarise key engagement activities with each department during the academic year and demonstrate how library services have supported each department's staff and students
- agree each department's strategic priorities and actions for the coming academic year in order to address specific issues or improve library services
- support departments with their annual and long-term strategic planning.

Action plan documents and data

The format of action plans has changed considerably over time in response to feedback and changing priorities and they have become increasingly nuanced for each department. They have also evolved from plain Word documents into highly visual PowerPoint files (shared with departments in PDF format).

Academic liaison librarians have full access to a range of data and key indicators for their departments, but the measures and statistics they choose to include in final action plan documents vary according to each department's needs and interests. As a general rule, academic liaison librarians use the data and metrics necessary to evidence the impact of their previous year's actions with their departments and to support their proposals for new actions for the year ahead. Action plans are therefore highly targeted to each department and action plan documents are written in a highly narrative style, to explain the data rather than just present it. This helps with a future distribution of the documents to academics who were not previously involved in action plan meetings where the data had been discussed in detail. There are three action plan document sections covering the year in summary, an update on the previous year, and details of proposed actions in the coming year.

Section 1: The year in summary

This section provides a top-level summary of departmental engagement and library activities over the previous year, including overall trends in activity and key indicative statistics, data or items to report. There is a statement about survey results for the department, drawing on overall satisfaction from the NSS, Postgraduate Taught Experience Survey (PTES; https://www.heacademy.ac.uk/institutions/surveys/postgraduate-taught-experience-survey), Postgraduate Research Experience Survey (PRES; https://www.heacademy.ac.uk/institutions/surveys/postgraduate-research-experience-survey) and LibQUAL+ surveys. The academic liaison librarians outline the strength of their relationship with the department, focusing on any particular changes or highlights over the previous year (e.g. attendance at a new departmental committee). This section ultimately sets out the content of the rest of the document and its overarching context.

Section 2: Update on previous year's actions

In this section, academic liaison librarians report back on the work they have done with the department over the previous year, evaluating its value and impact, and identifying what has changed as a result. They use data and feedback sources to help demonstrate this impact, for example including statistics on a particular department's use of the library's electronic texts (scanning) service where the original action was to improve overall use of that service by academic staff. Where possible, data is presented visually in the documents. Academic liaison librarians use a set of raw data provided to them in a master spreadsheet on Google Drive to create relevant graphs and charts. They draw on a number of key data sets to evidence their work in supporting departments over the previous year (older data is available through the University's central management information gateway):

- NSS satisfaction scores for the previous five years (including the overall departmental and library scores)
- PTES and PRES satisfaction scores for the previous two years (these surveys alternate each year)
- freshers' survey (new at York in 2016)
- LibQUAL+ satisfaction results for the last five years
- investment data (total spend per department on one-off and special purchases)
- books purchased in the two academic years previously and subsequently borrowed the following academic year (to understand more about how our purchasing policies work in practice)
- digitisation statistics
- borrowing statistics

- interlending statistics
- entry and exit turnstiles data
- digital skills teaching sessions
- one-to-one appointments with students
- subject guide usage statistics
- rate of departmental deposit into the research data repository at York, PURE
- uptake of ORCID (Research ID; https://orcid.org/).

Qualitative data is used alongside quantitative data to help describe particular engagement activities. For example, comments and feedback from students can be used to evidence the impact of changes to teaching skills that academic liaison librarians have implemented over the previous year. Comments by students and staff about gaps in the online and physical collections can highlight the impact of particular purchasing policies that have been set up. The key with qualitative data is to ensure that it is fully contextualised around specific actions or activities and is not presented out of context (or without context).

Progress updates are grouped in this section of the action plan document into three overarching themes: engagement, collections, and learning and teaching, with relevant data actively weaved throughout the narrative. Staff in some departments prefer data at a faculty rather than departmental level so they can understand how they compare with colleagues in similar fields. This information is provided initially in the action plan document and then further expanded at an action plan meeting.

Typically, the engagement section covers activities such as user experience projects that have taken place with departments, liaison between the department and the Library's Research Support Team, support with open days in departments, results from key user surveys (and qualitative comments in particular) and drop-ins that academic liaison librarians have run for students in departments.

The collections section includes information about individual departmental purchasing policies, major new acquisitions and subscriptions, and use of the Library's electronic texts service.

The final section on learning and teaching typically includes details of new, adapted and collaborative teaching sessions over the previous year, including any new materials that have been designed (and the take-up of these materials), appointments with students to discuss digital literacy skills and use of the online subject guides.

Section 3: New actions for the coming year

This section is structured into the same three headings as the previous section (engagement, collections, and learning and teaching) and sets out proposed new (SMART) actions for the coming year, drawing on relevant feedback and data to support those proposals. The academic liaison librarians carefully consider how each action will provide value for the department and have maximum impact on the staff and student experience. Two sample actions are described below.

Example 1
One of the large departments at York regularly spends its one-off resources allocation early on in the academic year, leaving little funding for additional purchases later in the year. At the 2016 action plan meeting, an action was agreed to understand more about how books purchased by staff and students for the department were subsequently used and whether a new purchasing policy would help to address budgetary issues. The research looked at borrowing statistics, digitisation requests and information on books used in the library but not borrowed. Over the coming year, the academic liaison librarian drew together data and evidence, working with academics to include more digitised readings on their resource lists rather than relying on multiple print copies, for example, and working with students to manage expectations about materials purchased to support wider topics. A new purchasing policy was established with the department, which has already significantly reduced the early spend in the academic year and helped to ensure that collection developed focuses on actual research and teaching needs.

Example 2
The University of York introduced the York Pedagogy in 2017, which aimed to set out a core set of programme learning outcomes for each undergraduate and postgraduate programme offered by the University. In preparation for implementing the York Pedagogy, the 2016 action plans included a commitment to start working with departments on developing and embedding digital skills support for particular programmes. Academic liaison librarians were subsequently involved in departmental discussions about programme and module changes and were able to update their digital skills training and support to students accordingly.

Action plan meetings and follow-up
Action plan meetings are held each academic year at the end of the spring term with the head of department, the academic library representative, the head of relationship management or the academic liaison team manager, and the academic liaison librarian for that department (who acts as chair). Draft action plan documents are circulated in advance of the meetings and then discussed and agreed at the action plan meetings themselves. The meetings are invaluable, not only in confirming what actions to prioritise for the coming year but in getting buy-in and support for those actions from departments. It is vital that the head of department, or another suitably senior representative (e.g. chair of board of studies), is present at the meeting so that actions can then be rolled out to departments with the full approval and support of senior managers. The action plan documents and meetings have contributed to an overall improvement in communications and engagement with academic departments, with the Library increasingly viewed as a

trusted partner in supporting departmental and university strategic priorities.

Following the meetings, overarching themes are identified and built into the year's strategic planning discussions across all teams in the Library. Academic liaison librarians start work on the new actions identified and record progress in a centralised spreadsheet, which links directly to the Library's in-house customer relationship management database and enables a holistic view of all activity taking place across all academic departments to be maintained.

Key insights

Action plans have provided an important insight into the strength of relationships between the Library and individual academic departments at York. Since their introduction, the documents have been redesigned and the action plan process itself modified to fit in with changing needs and expectations. Over the years, a number of insights have been gained into what constitutes a successful action plan and how libraries can implement them in order to maximise their value and impact. These are some key lessons learned:

- Action planning is a year-round process and requires individual ownership of that process. This ensures that a timetable of activities is in place, that all actions are followed through with departments, and that the plan is fully embedded within the academic liaison yearly workplan.
- Reliable data is essential and should be routinely and systematically collected throughout the year to assist with the writing of the annual action plan documents and to enable staff to respond to follow up queries throughout the year.
- Data on its own is rarely helpful; providing context and narrative on data leads to more meaningful and ultimately productive conversations with departments.
- Regular reporting on action plan progress to academic departments and within the library helps to demonstrate the value and impact of departmental engagement work.
- Universities are fast-changing environments and action plans need to be responsive and adaptable; continual review and improvement should be built into the process, drawing on regular, ongoing feedback from library and departmental staff.

Conclusions

Action plans are now fully embedded into the annual workplans for academic liaison librarians at York and will continue to be developed and refined over time. They have become a highly successful tool in ensuring that support for departments is tailored to individual needs, based on qualitative and quantitative evidence and measures. They demonstrate that library assessment goes beyond the production of metrics and data and can ultimately contribute to wider institutional strategic planning discussions and processes. In bringing together data with the wider, holistic departmental knowledge of liaison librarians, action planning can help to demonstrate the value of collaborative, partnership working between libraries and academic departments in support of the ambitious research and teaching agendas in universities today.

> **Case Study 8.2 University Library Services Sunderland: articulating value and impact through visual presentation of combined data sets**
> *Kay Grieves*

Introduction

The University of Sunderland has approximately 20,000 students based on campuses in Sunderland, London and Hong Kong and at global partnership institutions in 15 countries. The University has a long-established commitment to life-long learning, inclusivity and widening participation, and to acting as an agent of social change and opportunity. Sunderland is predominantly a teaching-focused institution, with an emphasis on a research-informed curriculum, delivered through diverse and flexible programmes.

University Library Services sits within the wider portfolio of Student Journey Services. On Sunderland Campus, library and study skill services are delivered through two campus libraries and innovative digital provision. The mission of Student Journey Services is to support and enable learners to get the very best from their University of Sunderland experience. It is a service with a culture of continuous improvement where staff, who are empowered to experiment, develop services and new ways of working. The library performance model is a powerful outcome of this culture and it now drives service design and delivery.

Our commitment to ensuring delivery of outcome-focused services and demonstrating the impact of those outcomes inspired us to design a new service and performance model, informed by strategic marketing theory. As Kotler and Armstrong say, 'The aim of marketing is to create value for customers and to capture value from customers in return' (2009, 26).

We wanted a service and performance model to inform our thinking and drive outcome-focused service design, while enabling the generation of targeted qualitative and quantitative evidence of engagement, outcome, value and impact. We hoped that applying strategic marketing theory would help us develop a new relationship with our customers, which through facilitated conversational opportunities enables them to understand the anticipated impact we could have on their academic success and wider experience of university, and nurtures them to articulate tangible evidence of their engagement and its impact.

We wanted a model that would realise the potential of qualitative, experiential outcome evidence and combine it with quantitative data sets to contextualise that output into meaningful, human stories. Lanclos describes this as 'constructing a compelling narrative . . . qualitative analytics such as ethnographical data are tailor made for the grounded storytelling in which libraries and other parts of higher education need to engage so as to draw resources and attention to their value' (2015, 108).

The service and performance model that we developed for the University Library Services Sunderland allows us to combine evidence sets and draw conclusions, which deepen understanding of our customers' experiences, our contribution to wider university objectives, the holistic outcomes we enable, and the value and impact of our services. It uses innovative approaches to data visualisation to package our evidence into powerful narratives that inform strategic conversations and advocacy with our stakeholders.

Applying the model to our assignment drop-in service: the six-step model

The model has six steps, demonstrated here using the example of how we supported students undertaking assignments in term 1 2015–16.

Step 1: Define the strategic objectives

Bookable, topic-based workshops were a key strand of our library skills offer. Few engaged with these workshops so we had a poor return on the amount of staff time involved. Out of 70 workshops offered over 2 terms, only 38 received bookings and were delivered. They were attended by 168 students and hosted by 2 liaison librarians. The average attendance across all of the sessions was 2.4 students. We also struggled with the concept and practicalities of capturing evidence of the long-term impact of these workshops on student experience and attainment. We focused instead on gathering reactive feedback on the delivery of the workshop or standalone services and products. Our 2015 strategic plan had the following objectives:

- to increase engagement with our skills offer and achieve effective value for money in time and cost
- to deepen our understanding of students' skills needs and wider university provision
- to gather evidence to articulate and demonstrate the value and impact of our study skills offer on the experience and attainment of our students.

Step 2: Define the expected outcomes, value and impact

In order to define our outcomes we ask ourselves, 'Why are we investing in this service? What do we want to come out of this service for our users?' (Hosseini-Ara and Jones, 2013, 2).

It is challenging to embed a performance culture with the focus on outcome for the customer, rather than on their satisfaction with products and services. It requires a focus on the effect of our services on the customer rather than purely the quality of those services and our delivery of them. It calls for us 'to embrace the "human" objectives, like success, happiness, productivity, progress, relationships, experiences and impact. How can we help users attain their goals, achieve wellbeing, realise benefits, move forward, make personal connections, participate fully and have significant effect on their worlds through us?' (Neal, 2011, 427). It also depends on the customer being positioned to recognise and explain how service engagement has added value or had an impact on them.

Our model addresses this challenge by building outcome into service design from the outset. We deliberately articulate and exemplify the anticipated outcomes of our service offers so that customers have a context against which to make a reflective value judgement about the actual outcome of those offers and their value and impact.

We wanted to provide:

- a holistic approach, where students receive blended and contextualised support, focused on their aspiration of writing an assignment rather than the previous generic, topic-led approach
- a triaged approach, where staff provided the skills-based solution to meet a student's need, as opposed to expecting students to identify which topic-based workshop to attend
- a one-off, drop-in format rather than the expectation to attend multiple 'book-only' workshops over a number of months.

The value and impact we expected to have was recognition by students that engagement with our skills offer had contributed positively to their experience of completing an assignment and to their attainment.

Step 3: Design a holistic service offer to achieve the outcomes
In designing a 'service offer' we blend services and products in order to deliver an identified outcome for a group of customers. Informed by our expected outcomes, we replaced our workshops with assignment drop-ins. The three-hour long drop-ins were held on four occasions in term 1. They were in a social space, facilitated by multiple library staff, who employed a triage approach.

Steps 4 and 5: Articulate the expected outcomes, value and impact of the service offer and plan how to generate and capture evidence of actual outcomes, value and impact
Our model achieves steps 4 and 5 through a campaign approach, which can be seen on the University of Sunderland Pinterest page (http://pinterest.com/uniofsunib). Through each campaign we encourage engagement by articulating the anticipated outcomes of our service offer. Having factored in time for engagement, we facilitate conversations with customers to encourage them to reflect and articulate the actual outcome, value and impacts of the services. During our assignment drop-in campaign we achieve this using specific techniques which we call 'facilitated conversations' undertaken through campus and social media interactions.

Crafting a 'rounded narrative' is how we describe our approach to combining evidence sets. The AMOSSHE Toolkit (2011) helped to inform this approach. This toolkit, which is being employed with powerful results in our Student Support Services Team, is designed to help student services professionals combine quantitative and qualitative data sets of inputs, outputs and outcomes to inform value judgements.

Through each campaign, we seek to facilitate conversations that will generate the quantitative and qualitative evidence sets we need to be able to combine our data into meaningful rounded narratives. During our drop-in campaign we generated:

- quantitative evidence of drop-in engagement collected through a triage process
- qualitative evidence of desired outcome and skill need collected through a triage process
- qualitative reaction evidence relating to satisfaction with the drop-in experience and anticipated outcome, value and impact collected through a feedback card at the end of a drop-in session
- qualitative, reflective evidence relating to the actual outcome, value and impact of our support on the experience of completing an assignment, invited at assignment submission through library displays, online forms and social media, with supplementary observations from academic and library staff.

Step 6: Collate, report and share evidence for maximum impact on stakeholders

The evidence we generate is collated and combined in order to articulate a meaningful 'story' for our stakeholders. Successful communication of these 'stories' relies largely on the tailored and targeted presentation of data. Data visualisation is therefore central to our model.

The infographic approach to data visualisation provides an effective alternative to written reports. Infographics enable us to structure our evidence sets into visual formats that are accessible and impactful. Online infographics allow us to showcase the human face and voice of evidence by incorporating dynamic media, e.g. video. Infographics can be shared with stakeholders in their entirety or used as a repository of evidence from which to draw relevant data. Our assignment drop-in evidence was collated into an online infographic (Grieves and Halpin, 2016).

As our collective evidence base of these rounded narratives expands (across the library and converged services within our wider Student Journey portfolio), we have the potential to combine the evidence within them in order to craft more inter-related and blended narratives, which better demonstrate the nature of our cross-service delivery. As we strive to deliver increasingly seamless and holistic outcomes, it becomes ever more imperative for us to enable stakeholders to recognise our 'invisible' contributions. Complex storytelling calls for ever more creative approaches to data visualisation 'that allows viewers to discover patterns that might otherwise be hard to uncover' (JISC, 2014).

With this in mind, in 2016 we re-imagined our approach to annual reporting. Our aim was to explain to the University executive how each of four service areas within the Student Journey portfolio had designed services that contributed to University objectives, showing evidence of engagement with those services and of their value and impact. Aware that our University executive was receptive to a graphical approach, we provided a single page data visualisation. Figure 8.1 shows the result, a design that illustrates our model, taken from the annual report for 2014–15. It depicts our strategic objectives at the centre, which lead to our key service offers. It then evidences engagement with those offers and gives powerful examples of their value and impact. The circular design highlights the holistic nature of our offers and ensures the reader can see a direct correlation between objective, service offer, engagement, value and impact.

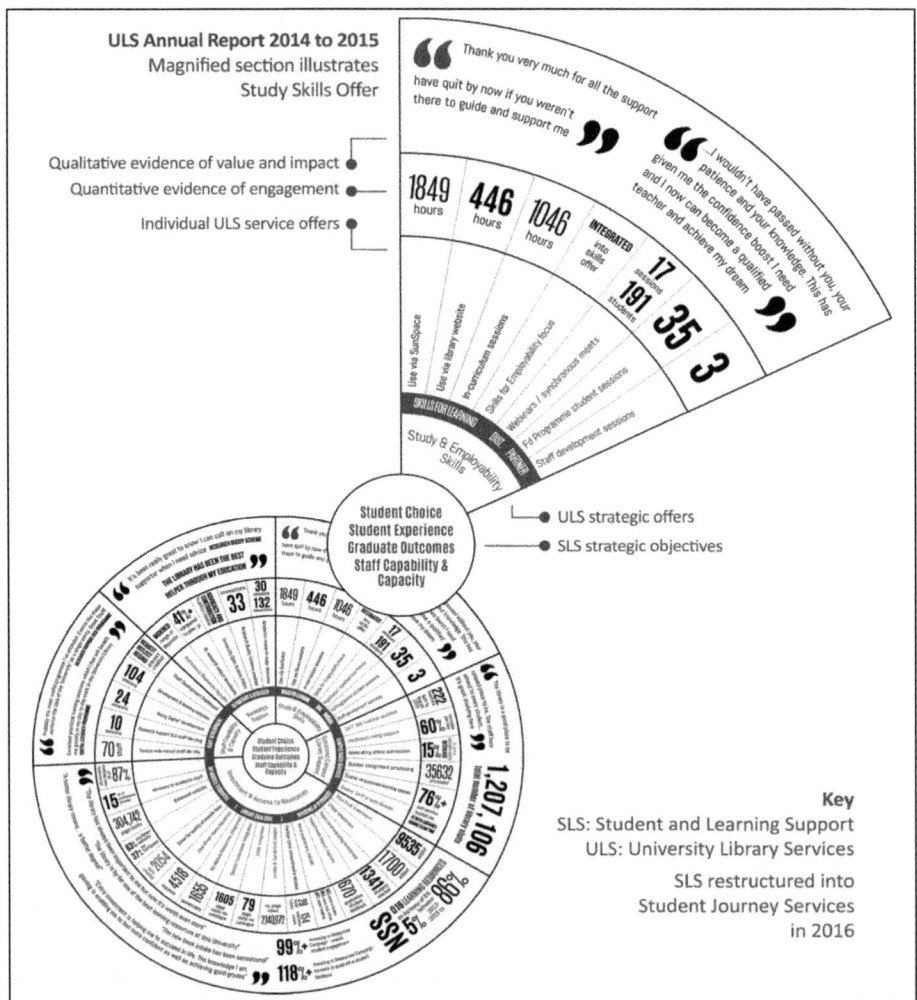

Figure 8.1 *Page from the University of Sunderland Library Services Annual Report 2014–15*

The University executive was very positive about our overall model and visual approach. We continue to innovate in this area and aim to further demonstrate the cross-service contributions of our converged services.

Outcomes of the assignment drop-in campaign

Following our campaign, student engagement with library workshops and their value for money (staff resource invested) increased, with a rise from 168 attendees at 38 sessions over a year to 90 attendees over 4 events in 1 term. This raised the average attendance per session from 2.4 to 22.5. The assignment drop-in format is now embedded for students living on campus and has been adapted for use in our partner colleges, improving student experience and providing value for money.

The evidence provided us with a deeper understanding of the study skill needs of our students and the variability between faculty and subject disciplines. Of particular note was the lack of differentiation in students' perception between 'library' and 'study' skills. They expected the library to have a role in delivering both and demand was highest for 'study' rather than 'library' skill topics. This evidence supported our decision to take a holistic, outcome-based approach to our assignment drop-ins. The qualitative evidence regarding the value and impact of our service offer was effective and highly valuable in informing core messages to promote future drop-ins and encourage further engagement.

Our deeper understanding informed advocacy with members of the University executive, which further raised their awareness of student need and skills provision in the library and faculty. It informed data-driven decisions around provision and resource, which contributed to significant service change. In 2017 university study skills support was centralised within library services and a team of faculty study skill advisers were relocated to the Library in order to deliver a holistic skills service in partnership with the Liaison Librarian Team. This new approach was driven by a published study skills offer that centres largely on the drop-in approach.

Conclusions

Our service delivery and performance model has provided a transferable framework with which we can inform service design to meet our strategic service objectives and achieve our expected outcomes.

The initial building of outcome into service design enables us to generate targeted snapshots of evidence, which when combined into 'rounded narratives' provide authentic 'stories' that resonate with our customers. As the model produces an ever-increasing evidence base of specific 'rounded narratives' they too can be synthesised to develop narratives which evidence cross-service, holistic outcomes that may otherwise be invisible.

Through our innovative approaches to data visualisation we are able to craft these narratives into tailored reports for our different stakeholders. They enable us to demonstrate the outcomes of service engagement and deepen understanding of our impact and value, thereby informing influential conversations and advocacy with our stakeholders and enhancing service visibility and reputation.

Conclusions

The two case studies in this chapter demonstrate how bringing together a variety of sources of data and feedback enables a library to acquire a deeper understanding of users' needs and the impact of service changes, and to tell the story of the library service in a meaningful way. The case studies show that taking care to ensure the appropriateness of the medium of communicating the message is as important as the message itself in achieving successful advocacy for the library service.

References

AMOSSHE (2011) *Value and Impact Toolkit*, www.amosshe.org.uk.

Cox, B. L. and Jantti, M. H. (2012) Capturing Business Intelligence Required for Targeted Marketing, Demonstrating Value, and Driving Process Improvement, *Library and Information Science Research*, **34**, 308–16.

Creswell, J. W. and Plano Clark, V. L. (2011) *Designing and Conducting Mixed Methods Research*, Sage.

Deming, W. E. (2000) *Out of the Crisis*, MIT Press.

Few, S. (2013) Data Visualization for Human Perception. In Soegaard, M. and Dam, R. F. (eds), *Encyclopedia of human-computer interaction*, Interactive Design Foundation.

Grieves, K. and Halpin, M. (2016) *Assignment Drop-in Term 1 2016*, https://magic.piktochart.com/output/13597669-growing-assignment-skills-2016.

Hosseini-Ara, M. Jones, R. (2013) Overcoming Our Habits and Learning to Measure Impact, *Computers in Libraries*, **33** (5), 3–7.

JISC (2014) *Data Visualization*, www.jisc.ac.uk/guides/data-visualisation.

Kean, D. (2016) UK Library Budgets fall by £25m in a Year, *Guardian*, 8 December, www.theguardian.com/books/2016/dec/08/uk-library-budgets-fall-by-25m-in-a-year.

Kotler, P. and Armstrong, G. (2009) *Principles of Marketing*, 13th edn, Prentice Hall.

Lanclos, D. (2015) Going Beyond Numbers. In Showers, B. (ed.), *Library Analytics and Metrics*, Facet Publishing.

Neal, J. G. (2011) Stop the Madness: the insanity of ROI and the need for new qualitative measures, in *Academic Library Success: proceedings of an international conference held on March 30–April 2, 2011, organized by the Association of College*

and Research Libraries (ARCL), Philadelphia, Pennsylvania,
www.ala.org/acrl/sites/ala.org.acrl/files/content/conferences/confsandpreconfs/
national/2011/papers/stop_the_madness.pdf.

Oxford English Dictionary (2011) 3rd edn, Oxford University Press.

Smith, D., Schlaepfer, P., Major, K., Dyble, M., Page, A. E., Thompson, J., Chaudhary,
N., Salali, G. D., Mace, R., Astete, A., Ngales, M., Vinivius, L. and Migliano, A. B.
(2017) Cooperation and the Evolution of Hunter-Gatherer Storytelling, *Nature
Communications*, **8**, 1853.

Chapter 9

Conclusions

We hope this book has given you the basics you need to apply a variety of assessment methodologies in your library. You may wish to use institutional measures of customer satisfaction to advocate for the library with senior institutional administrators – as evidence of the impact of library provision on the customer experience and/or to argue for the necessary resources to make improvements.

Alternatively you may want to use the results of a standardised library survey to benchmark against others to identify your library's strengths and opportunities for improvement. Or maybe responses to an in-house library survey could help you understand your customers' needs and what actions your library staff need to take to improve their experience.

Maybe you have a plethora of library data sets, such as circulation statistics, that you want to use to inform decision making and service planning.

Perhaps it is qualitative feedback that you have collected and now wish to harness to gain understanding and insight into your customers' interactions with your library, and thereby make improvements. Or you now realise that data is an encompassing term for both quantitative and qualitative information, and they must be used in combination for your library to have a complete understanding of the matter.

Or maybe you have made full use of all the data you have and there is still something missing, so you are inspired to apply an emerging technique in library assessment at your library.

We hope the case studies have inspired you and shown how the theory works in the real world. We hope that after reading this book you will bring together a variety of sources of data and feedback to give your library a deeper understanding of users' needs and the impact of service changes, thereby continually improving customers' experience. We hope that you will use the same data, carefully communicated, to tell the story of your library service in a meaningful way and so secure future funding.

Culture shift

When case study authors or presenters at library assessment conferences provide the context for their library, the default of even the enthusiastic few at the cutting edge of this area is to provide statistics about the size of their collections and the population they serve. We are guilty of this behaviour ourselves. Despite the trend from focusing on size to now concentrating on satisfaction rates and impact, librarians still revert to quantifying their stock as a way of describing their services.

This is a problem because libraries have a finite amount of time to devote to assessment work. If most of that time is spent counting things – usually because national statistics bodies such as the Society of College, National and University Libraries (SCONUL), the Association of Research Libraries (ARL) and the Canadian Association of Research Libraries require them to do so – there is no time left to spend on using library data to improve library services.

One way to square this circle is for library staff to use the input and output data they collect to assess and improve their libraries, thereby enabling them to see a return on their investment of staff time, but they appear to struggle to do this. When seeking case studies for this book, we were unable to identify anyone either in the literature or through the library assessment community who is using national statistics sets to improve their library service. The primary use we have identified has been by ARL libraries using their statistics to state their position in a league table as a publicity claim. This practice is not common in the UK and when conducting the literature review we found limited examples of how SCONUL data is actually used by libraries, or the national body.

As the proverb states: what gets measured gets done. Therefore, the only way to change the culture of libraries from counting inputs and outputs to assessing satisfaction and impact is for the national bodies to gather data on satisfaction and impact, and stop collecting 'library statistics'. Between 2014 and 2017 Research Libraries UK tried to do this by gathering data on service standard attainment (Stanley and Knowles, 2016). However, the 'SCONUL statistics' still had to be provided, so this was not sufficient to cause a shift in emphasis. While collecting these statistics is not mandatory there appears to be a culture of counting, as it is what we have always done.

Our focus in this book has been to look at how library data can and has been used to improve the library. We advocate that all library assessment activities should be useful and used – if you are not going to use the data, don't ask the question. Libraries do not appear to be using the data they submit to national bodies, so perhaps the national bodies should stop asking those questions.

Putting library assessment data to work

Why should you make the effort and your library staff invest the time in doing more than collecting the necessary library statistics? For us, it's about fostering a continual improvement culture, grounded in customers' expectations, 'customers' being an inclusive term for users, readers, paymasters, senior stakeholders, governance and community. We are a service industry. If we are not going to provide what our customers want from us we will become obsolete and eventually redundant (Wilson, 2006). As Deming so succinctly put it, 'You do not have to do these things. Survival is not compulsory' (1986, 17).

The core ethos of this book is that good enough is good enough. It is better to do something than continually quest for perfection and so do nothing. Perfect data is unattainable because of technical, financial or ethical barriers. You may feel that you lack the time, money, skills or confidence to undertake library assessment. Hopefully this book has addressed the last two of these issues, and demonstrated that the first two need not be barriers to undertaking worthwhile assessment.

So go on – dust off that data sitting on the 'shelf' and put it to work. Your customers will be glad you did.

References

Deming, W. E. (1986) *Out of the Crisis: quality, productivity and competitive position*, Cambridge University Press.

Stanley, T. and Knowles, J. (2016) Demonstrating Value in Research Libraries: the shared service standards initiative, *Performance Measurement and Metrics*, **17**, 188–93.

Wilson, L. (2006) Seattle to Charlottesville and Back Again: building a library assessment community. In DeFranco, F. et al. (eds), *Library Assessment Conference*, Association of Research Libraries, 449–52, http://libraryassessment.org/bm~doc/proceedings-lac-2006.pdf.

Index